OFFSHORING IT

THE GOOD, THE BAD, AND THE UGLY

Bill Blunden

APress Media, LLC

Offshoring IT: The Good, the Bad, and the Ugly

Originally published by Apress in 2004
MyCopy version of the original edition 2004

Library of Congress Cataloging-in-Publication Data

Blunden, Bill, 1969-
Offshoring IT : the good, the bad, and the ugly / Bill Blunden.
p. cm.
Includes index.

DOI 10.1007/978-1-4302-0740-5
1. Information technology--Management. 2. Contracting out. I. Title.

HD30.2.B58 2004
004'.068'4--dc22

2004014679

In the United States: phone 1-800-SPRINGER, e-mail orders@springer-ny.com, or visit http://www.springer-ny.com. Outside the United States: fax +49 6221 345229, e-mail orders@springer.de, or visit http://www.springer.de.

For information on translations, please contact Apress directly at 2560 Ninth Street, Suite 219, Berkeley, CA 94710. Phone 510-549-5930, fax 510-549-5939, e-mail info@apress.com, or visit http://www.apress.com.

This book is dedicated to my primary sources:

The U.S. Federal Reserve System
The Bureau of Labor Statistics
The National Center for Education Statistics
The Bureau of the U.S. Census
The Department of Homeland Security

Contents at a Glance

Contents

About the Author

Reverend Bill Blunden is an alumnus of Cornell University, where he earned a bachelor of arts degree in physics. He also holds a master of science degree in operations research from Case Western Reserve. Reverend Blunden is an ordained SubGenius minister and is currently at large in the East Bay.

Acknowledgments

This book required a certain degree of willpower and devotion. That's a nice way of saying obsession, my forte. If I am able to do one thing, it is to single-mindedly set my mind to something, to submerge myself in carefully directed thought. Yet, I couldn't have finished this book without the help of several people.

I would like to thank all the people at Apress who encouraged me and put up with my shenanigans. Specifically, I would like to thank the Big Kahuna himself, Gary Cornell, for giving me the opportunity to write for Apress. I would also like to thank my editor, Jim Sumser, who has worked tirelessly to send this book to print. Jim knew that this was my book; that of all the potential authors, I was the one with the most fervent beliefs and the gnawing desire to expound on them.

There are many people at Apress who labor anonymously in the background to get things done, and I owe them a debt of gratitude. This includes people like Ami Knox, Sofia Marchant, Kelly Winquist, Dina Quan, Katie Stence, Kevin Broccoli, Kurt Krames, and Tom Debolski.

I would specifically like to extend my thanks to Professor Claus Hofhansel for agreeing to review the initial manuscript. Roughly fourteen years ago, Claus was grading a 10-page term paper that I wrote for his class on international relations. Karma has brought my old instructor back once again to serve as a rational counterbalance of sorts.

Noam Chomsky has had a very strong influence on the development of my worldview. He is a voice of conscience in a nation whose foreign and domestic policies don't always reflect the best interests of the general public. Chomsky's gift is to show us that we should take nothing for granted, that we should learn how to identify and challenge underlying assumptions.

I would also like to thank Rick Chapman, my main man in Connecticut.

Finally, I would like to thank Robert G. Morgan for taking the back cover photograph, Lance Morgan for reading my long-winded diatribes, and Ronan Morgan for periodically inviting me up to Glen Ellen.

Praise Bob,
Reverend Bill Blunden
Church of the SubGenius

Preface

Offshoring is an emotional topic, and one is sorely tempted to rant. I have strong feelings about the subject, as do hundreds of thousands of other white-collar professionals in the U.S. This isn't a historical trend that's been archived in high school textbooks; it's a development that's right here in front of our faces. Offshoring has the potential to change the very nature of our economy, for better or for worse.

Therein lies the question: will it make us better off over the long run, or send us careening into a terminal period of violent class warfare?

If you're a corporate executive, offshoring looks like a nifty way to decrease cost structure. If you're a not an executive, offshoring looks like a one-way ticket to the poor house. Each side feels that it can justify its position with credible arguments. Each side can go on and on for hours about Adam Smith's invisible hand or the questionable ethics of laissez faire economics. My job, as a researcher, is to dig out the facts and connect the dots, so to speak. Or, to let you connect them for yourself if you're so inclined.

There's an old story about how Greek philosophers sat around debating about how many teeth a horse has. When you want to know how many teeth a horse has, nothing beats looking a horse in the mouth. Don't take someone else's word for it. Thus, I spent much of my time hunkered down with government studies. Whenever possible, I've tried to cite my sources specifically so that you can easily verify data for yourself.

There is a darker side to ambiguity, beyond sheer laziness. Which is to say that some people are intentionally vague with the hope that you'll simply take their word for it. They wave their hands in they air with the guarded expectation that you'll take everything they say at face value. I won't try to insult your intelligence in this manner.

Finally, the thing about questions is that they lead to other questions. When I started to research this book, I intended to answer a small handful of fairly straightforward questions: Who's going offshore? Who stands to benefit? What are the potential long-term effects? What I discovered was that the subject of offshoring led me to pose deeper, more fundamental questions about our economic system and this country's class structure. The conclusions that I reached disturbed me. Simply put, the system has been rigged to benefit a tiny group of economically privileged citizens. They stand to gain from offshore outsourcing and the rest of us stand to lose.

CHAPTER 1

Setting the Stage

Chapter at a Glance

- ▶ Labor and Capital
- ▶ Outsourcing
  - ▶ H-1B Backgrounder
  - ▶ The L-1 Option
  - ▶ L-1 Visa Fallout
- ▶ Noncitizen Students in the U.S.
- ▶ The Cost of Education in the U.S.
- ▶ Offshoring and Manufacturing
- ▶ The Software Industry Matures
- ▶ Third-World Development
- ▶ The Bottom Line ($$$)

What's going on . . . is the end of Silicon Valley as we know it.

—Larry Ellison, *Wall Street Journal*, April 8, 2003

Although human reactions like fear and greed may prohibit accurate short-term forecasts, over the long run the fundamental axioms of economics hold sway. Inevitably, the market obeys the laws of supply and demand (sometimes it just takes a while). Thus, to gain insight into the enduring implications of offshoring, it may be helpful to take a look at a few basic economic concepts.

Have no fear—I will keep my discussion to a bare minimum. I won't stuff differential equations down your throat or assail you with equilibrium charts. For the most part, the economics of offshoring aren't sophisticated;

they're trivial. Father Guido Sarducci once stated that he could teach you, in five minutes, everything about economics that the average college student remembered a year after graduation:

> *Economics, is a' simple . . . is a' supply and a' demand.*

Labor and Capital

Labor and capital are essential ingredients of an economy. Nothing could happen without them. Back in the 1700s, *capital* (I'm using the financial definition, as in wealth) was relatively fixed. The digital communication infrastructure that we have today, to move assets around the globe, didn't exist. If you wanted to move raw currency, it could take weeks to travel a few hundred miles by horse. Furthermore, wealth was often accumulated in terms of land ownership (i.e., *natural capital*), which is immobile by nature.

Labor, on the other hand, was mobile. Plague, famine, and poverty forced people to abandon familiar surroundings and migrate en masse to someplace else. If living conditions went to hell for whatever reason, the peasant folk could always pick up and move. Life was brutal during the eighteenth century.

Such was the state of affairs in 1798, when Thomas Malthus wrote *An Essay on the Principle of Population*, a depressing book that spelled out what economists now refer to as the *Malthusian Doctrine*. According to Malthus, because land is fixed and populations grow at a geometric rate, eventually a population will overwhelm the land that once sustained it. This will inevitably lead to shortages, starvation, and death (which serve as Mother Nature's population regulators). His pessimistic outlook is one reason why economics is called *the dismal science*.[1]

Just because it's old doesn't mean that Malthusian Doctrine isn't relevant. Peak Oil theorists predict that the world's production of oil will peak sometime between the years 2000 and 2010. From that point onward, the supply will eventually dwindle to a trickle such that the demand for oil will dwarf the available supply. Researchers like Richard Heinberg[2] believe that the end result will be doomsday: a horrific Malthusian apocalypse in which 90 percent of the population perishes.

In a report the U.S. Department of Defense commissioned in 2003,[3] the authors concluded that changes in the world's climate could pose the greatest single threat to national security in the coming century. Specifically, the report suggested that global warming could lead to a "slowing of the ocean's

---

[1] *David Colander,* Macroeconomics *(Scott, Foresman and Company, 1986)*

[2] *Richard Heinberg,* The Party's Over: Oil, War and the Fate of Industrial Societies *(New Society Publishers, 2003)*

[3] *Peter Schwartz and Doug Randall,* An Abrupt Climate Change Scenario and Its Implications for United States National Security *(commissioned by the U.S. Department of Defense, 2003)*

thermohaline conveyor," resulting in catastrophic alterations in our climate patterns and worldwide famine—in other words, a Malthusian die-off of staggering proportions.

With the development of a global financial system and immigration laws, the relative mobility of capital and labor has been inverted. Capital is now mobile, even more so than labor. Today it's trivial to wire a billion dollars across the planet, but it's also well nigh impossible to move the entire population of one country into another. The relative mobility of capital, vis-à-vis the global banking system, coupled with the development of a worldwide information network has given American corporations the opportunity to turn the international labor pool into a market such that they can select the most inexpensive alternative from a number of competing labor providers. *Corporations are now free to move between countries, playing one country's workforce against another to obtain the cheapest possible labor.*

Steven Roach, the chief economist and director of global economic analysis at Morgan Stanley, has aptly referred to this phenomenon as *global labor arbitrage.*[4]

In finance, *risk arbitrage* is the practice of buying a commodity at a low price in one market and then selling it for a high price in another market. Ivan Boesky, who was indicted for insider trading with Michael Milken in the 1980s, got his start in risk arbitrage.[5] An arbitrageur is essentially a person who has discovered a money machine. Theoretically, the markets are supposed to be "efficient," such that price differentials between markets don't exist. In practice, pockets of inefficiency exist. This is why offshore outsourcing is referred to as global labor arbitrage. Labor is being bought in one market at a low price, and being utilized in another market where it has a higher value.

Outsourcing

In order for an international labor market to exist, there have to be *alternative sources*. Back in the 1950s and 1960s, there was only one source. U.S. corporations didn't have any choice; the global communication networks were tenuous at best. In America, they had to hire American workers. In the 1960s, software engineering was considered a solid career path, and COBOL was a cutting-edge technology. At cocktail parties, you could hold your head up high and tell people that you were a programmer. Programmers were in demand; they had respect.

Today, if you tell people you're a programmer, they'll ask you how long you have until your unemployment benefits run out.

[4] *Stephen Roach, "The Global Labor Arbitrage,"* Global Economic Forum *(Morgan Stanley, October 6, 2003)*

[5] *James B. Stewart,* Den of Thieves *(Simon & Schuster, 1992)*

There are immigration laws in place in the U.S. and a plethora of federal organizations to prevent *large-scale* immigration. In this day and age, you'd never see the entire population of one country move into another, although you might see a large chunk of a nation's population move around within its borders. For example, the U.S. Census Bureau reports that half of the American population moved between 1995 and 2000 . . . it's just that they all stayed within the confines of the U.S.[6] If those people had moved to Canada or Mexico, it would be a different story.

Despite the legal barriers that hinder the migration of a population en masse, loopholes exist that corporations can use to allow for labor-based immigration on a smaller scale. This has provided American corporations with the alternative they need to create an international labor market. Specifically, I'm talking about outsourcing.

Outsourcing is a practice whereby an external agency is hired to provide services to a company that could normally be performed in-house. In the U.S., the H-1B and L-1 visa programs facilitate outsourcing. A number of outsource service providers like Tata Consultancy Services, Wipro Ltd. (NYSE: WIT), and Infosys Technologies Ltd. (NYSE: INFY) recruit workers in other countries on behalf of U.S. employers, who then sponsor their visas.

The *Immigration and Nationality Act* (INA) spells out the foundation of our immigration laws. The INA was created in 1952, though it has been amended several times.[7] For example, the *America Competitiveness in the Twenty-First Century Act*, or AC21 (Public Law 106-313), which was signed by President Clinton in 2000, made amendments to the INA.

NOTE The INA is subset of the *U.S. Code*, which contains the same material under title 8, *Aliens and Nationality* (U.S.C. 8).

H-1B Backgrounder

The *Immigration Act of 1990* (Public Law 101-649) amends the INA. Section 205 of this act establishes the H-1B nonimmigrant visa category. The H-1B category denotes temporary workers who have specialty occupations, are employed by the DoD, or are employed as fashion models.[8] The H-1B program was initially created to help businesses to deal with labor shortages, although the very nature of a "shortage" of labor in the software industry is dubious. Which is to say that high-tech employers have allegedly used the idea of labor shortage as an excuse to import cheaper foreign labor instead of using local American talent.

---

[6] *U.S. Census Bureau, Public Information Office news release (September 23, 2003,* `http://www.census.gov/Press-Release/www/releases/archives/census_2000/001387.html`*)*

[7] `http://uscis.gov/graphics/lawsregs/INA.htm`

[8] `http://uscis.gov/graphics/services/visas.htm`

What Labor Shortage?

According to researchers like Peter Cappelli, the director of Wharton's Center for Human Resources, the U.S. won't face a shortage of workers in the coming years. In his 2003 study, "Will There *Really* Be a Labor Shortage?"[9] he claims that the real problem will be retention. With baby boomers hanging onto their careers, and an increase in the number of college graduates, there will be a large pool of available candidates. If companies encounter hurdles with regard to hiring new employees, it will be due to changes in employee-employer relations that make it harder to retain good workers. According to Cappelli, "There's no good argument for sustaining the view that we have to expand immigration because there is no basis to the view that there aren't enough people to fill jobs."

In 2000, during the dot-com boom, the AC21 temporarily lifted the annual H-1B ceiling to 195,000 after being lobbied by the high-tech industry. On October 1, 2003, the ceiling was lowered back down to 65,000 (see section 102, "Temporary Increase in Visa Allotments").

An H-1B visa holder can remain in the U.S. for up to six years and must be paid the *prevailing industry wage* (see *U.S. Code* subsection 1182(n)(1)(a)). The AC21 provides for extensions in a couple of cases (see sections 104(c) and 106(a)). Prevailing wage information can be found in the *Occupational Employment Statistics* (OES) survey compiled by the Bureau of Labor Statistics, although the exact legal definition leaves room for interpretation.

According to the *American Competitiveness and Workforce Improvement Act of 1998*, or ACWIA (Public Law 105-277), H-1B visa holders can't be used to displace American workers. For instance, H-1B employees can't be used to break a strike or be hired immediately after American workers are laid off. However, this does *not* necessarily mean that employers will choose American workers over H-1B workers, if given the choice.

The ambiguous nature of a prevailing wage has come under scrutiny. Recently I spoke with Norman Matloff, a professor in the Computer Science Department at University of California Davis, about the H-1B laws.

Matloff asserts

> *Actually, none of those things really matters. The wage floor for H-1B is a sham, with a ton of loopholes that make the prevailing-wage portion of the law meaningless. Similarly, the H-1B visa cap has never been a genuine constraint either, because Congress always increases the cap whenever the industry wants it.*

[9] Organizational Dynamics *32, no. 3 (August 2003): pp. 221–318*

David Lazarus, a columnist for the *San Francisco Chronicle*, looked into some of these loopholes.[10] For example, Lazarus discovered that prevailing wage abuses are only investigated after an H-1B employee has lodged a formal complaint. Most H-1B workers, who are dependent upon their employers for their H-1B status, are too scared to come forward. According to John Fraser, deputy administrator of the Department of Labor's Wage and Hour division, "The notion that this program can be enforced on a complaint-only basis is naive, if not misguided."[11]

The L-1 Option

As an alternative to importing H-1B workers, companies can rely on the more obscure L-1 visa program. The L-1 visa classification, which was introduced by an amending act in April 1970, was intended to help multinational corporations with intracompany transfers.

The L-1 program doesn't bar employers from displacing American workers, and L-1 visa employees don't have to be paid the prevailing wage. More importantly, there is also no upper limit with respect to the number of L-1 workers that can be brought into the U.S. L-1 visa holders can stay in the U.S. for up to seven years if they are managers and five years if they have "specialized knowledge."

The Bureau of Labor Statistics, in its January 2004 *Employment Situation Summary*,[12] reported that the working population of the U.S. consists of roughly 147 million people. Of those, the 2002 *Occupational Employment Statistics* report says that over 2.7 million are in the software industry (i.e., Standard Occupational Classification 150-0000, Computer and Mathematical Science Occupations).

The 2002 *Yearbook of Immigration Statistics*, published by the Office of Immigration Statistics (under the Department of Homeland Security), reports that the number of H-1B and L-1 visa *admissions* in the U.S. is approximately 684,189 (see Table 1-1).

Table 1-1 L-1 and H-1B Admissions

Year	L-1 Admissions	H-1B Admissions
1985	65,349	47,322
1990	63,180	100,446
1995	112,124	117,574
1999	234,443	302,326

[10] *David Lazarus, "A Question of Fraud: Silicon Valley Pushes for More Foreign Workers,"* San Francisco Chronicle *(September 21, 2000)*

[11] *Ibid.*

[12] `http://www.bls.gov/news.release/empsit.nr0.htm`

Year	L-1 Admissions	H-1B Admissions
2000	294,658	355,605
2001	328,480	384,191
2002	313,699	370,490

Source: 2002 Yearbook of Immigration Statistics

NOTE When visa holders leave the country and then reenter the U.S., they are counted again as an admission. This results in a certain amount of admission redundancy, such that the number you see for H-1B admissions are over the ceilings that I mentioned previously.

According to an official whom I spoke with at the Department of Homeland Security, the U.S. government as of January 2004 *doesn't know how exactly many H-1B and L-1 visa holders there are in the U.S.* This is due to the fact that they don't know how many petitions correspond to a unique individual. In some cases, different companies may petition for the same individual, or a company may file multiple petitions for the same individual. The point is this: anyone who tells you how many H-1B or L-1 visa holders there are in the U.S. is speculating, or full of it. Period.

According to the *2002 Yearbook of Immigration Statistics,* there were 215,000 H-1B petitions filed in 2002. Of these, 198,000 H-1B visas were approved (104,000 of which were for initial employment, the rest were for extensions). Table 1-2 breaks this down according to country. As you can see, approximately 33 percent of the petitions were from India.

Table 1-2 H-1B Petitions In 2002

Country	Beneficiaries	Median Age	Median Income
India	64,980	29	60,000
China	18,841	32	48,000
Canada	11,760	34	70,000
Philippines	9,295	32	38,000
U.K.	7,171	33	68,000
Korea	5,941	34	42,000
Japan	4,937	31	38,000
Taiwan	4025	31	42,000
Pakistan	3810	31	50,000
Columbia	3320	32	38,000

Source: 2002 Yearbook of Immigration Statistics

Obviously, a steady stream of noncitizen workers is being let into the U.S. through a back door. The L-1 visa category, in particular, is an insidious loophole simply because not many people know about it. One of the reasons that I've written this book is to publicize programs like L-1 and how they are exploited.

L-1 Visa Fallout

The utilization of the L-1 visa program in practice has come under scrutiny. U.S. Senator Dianne Feinstein (D-California) claims that the L-1 visa program is nothing more than "stealth immigration" that is stealing jobs from American workers.[13]

Corporations like Siemens Information Communication Networks (ICN) have been accused of using L-1 workers to replace American employees. In the winter of 2002, an engineer named Mike Emmons was let go by Siemens ICN after the company decided to outsource his entire department. In addition to losing his $90,000 salary, Mike was offered a modest severance package (up to $13,000) if he agreed to stay on and teach his replacements.[14]

> **NOTE** Can you imagine being forced to dig your own grave? Talk about adding insult to injury! Having American workers train their imported replacements seems to be in fashion these days. Patricia Fluno, one of Mike's coworkers at Siemens who was forced to help her replacement climb the learning curve, called it "humiliating."[15] Bob Simoni, a 39-year-old software engineer who lost his job at Toshiba America in 2002, was also required to train his replacement.[16] So was Phil Marraffinni, an engineer at First Data Corporation, who lost his job in 2002.[17] According to Marraffinni, "I had to give classes. And I wasn't the only one." One engineer at Bank of America, Kevin Flanagan, was so upset by losing his job after training his replacements that he shot himself dead in the parking lot outside of B of A's Concord Technology Center.[18]

Boy, did Siemens mess with the wrong guy! Emmons, a normally well-behaved suburbanite and father of two, went on the warpath.[19] He landed spots on CNN and *ABC World News Tonight*, and now Mike is running for Congress in Florida's seventh district.

---

[13] *Roy Mark, "High Tech Worker Visas Come Under Fire,"* internetnews.com *(July 30, 2003,* `http://www.internetnews.com/ec-news/article.php/2242281`*)*

[14] *Ben Worthen, "The Radicalization of Mike Emmons,"* CIO Magazine *(September 1, 2003)*

[15] *Carolyn Lochhead, "Feinstein Seeking Changes in Skilled-Worker Visas,"* San Francisco Chronicle *(July 30, 2003)*

[16] *Spencer Ante and Paul Magnusson, "Too Many Visas for Techies?"* Business Week *(August 11, 2003)*

[17] *"Imported Workers Filling U.S. Jobs,"* CBS News *(October 22, 2003)*

[18] *William F. Jasper, "Trading Away Jobs and Liberty,"* New American *(June 30, 2003)*

[19] `http://www.outsourcecongress.org:81`

Emmons says

> *I believe that powerful special interests in Washington are using illegal immigration and foreign work visa programs to drive down the wages of Americans, thus creating greater gains for influential corporations. It is collusion between corporations that pour big money into politics and Congress that passes legislation enabling the corporations to replace American workers with substitutes, thereby keeping all wages artificially low to increase corporate profits.*

Mike's not just whistling Dixie. Florida congressman John L. Mica spoke with Emmons in September 2002, giving him the impression that he'd look into the problem of L-1 immigration. Later on, a watchdog organization in Washington, D.C., the Center for Responsive Politics, reports that Mica received $3,999 in donations from Siemens between the time that Emmons first contacted him in August 2002 and the following November elections.[20]

Noncitizen Students in the U.S.

One thing that exacerbates the availability of alternative labor sources is the relative increase in the number of international students enrolled in U.S. colleges and universities. Foreign countries, having an appreciation for their own educational shortcomings, have been leveraging the U.S. system for the last few decades. The United States has the world's preeminent collection of research universities (e.g., Caltech, Princeton, MIT). It's no surprise then that foreign governments encourage their citizens to attend. Lasting economic growth, in the modern world, is a function of having an educated workforce. Developing countries understand that it's in their best interest to absorb every bit of knowledge that they can from the most powerful nation on the planet.

Over the past couple of decades, the number of foreign students receiving advanced degrees from American institutions has dramatically increased. According to the National Center for Education Statistics (NCES),[21] which compiled the 2002 *Digest of Education Statistics*, approximately 28 percent of the students who were awarded Ph.D.s in 2000 were non-U.S. citizens. Over 38 percent of the physical science Ph.D.s who graduated in 2000 were non-U.S. citizens, and over 47 percent of the mathematics Ph.D.s who graduated in 2000 were non-U.S. citizens.

---

[20] *Ben Worthen, "The Radicalization of Mike Emmons,"* CIO Magazine *(September 1, 2003)*

[21] *U.S. Department of Education, National Center for Education Statistics,* Digest of Education Statistics *(2002): Table 298*

As far as outsourcing is concerned, this is salient. To understand the true significance of this development, look at the percentage of noncitizen physical science Ph.D.s going back to 1980 in Table 1-3.[22]

Table 1-3 Noncitizen Physical Science Ph.D.s

Year	Percentage Non-U.S. Ph.D.s
1979–80	21.6
1980–81	21.3
1985–86	27.8
1988–89	29.8
1989–90	32.4
1990–91	35.9
1991–92	39.6
1992–93	39.7
1993–94	41.7
1994–95	41.7
1995–96	41.8
1996–97	36.3
1997–98	36.4
1998–99	37.9
1999–2000	38.2

Source: Digest of Education Statistics *(2002): Table 303*

As you can see, the number of non-U.S. citizens who were awarded Ph.D.s basically doubled from the level that existed back when Ronald Reagan was in office. It may help to see this data graphically (refer to Figure 1-1).

It's getting to the point where American students are in the minority at graduate programs in the U.S. During my two years of graduate school, at Case Western Reserve's Department of Operations Research, American students were a contingent of the department's composition.

NOTE I have nothing against students from other countries. What I'm trying to illustrate is how quickly emerging countries are catching up with us, and how dire the situation is. The technological lead that we possessed after World War II is all but gone.

[22]*Ibid.:Table 303*

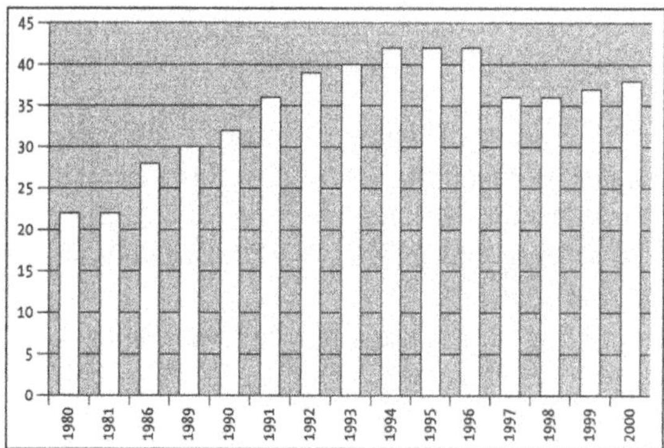

Figure 1-1 Graph of data in Table 1-3

Upon graduation, students from abroad can either try to land a visa here in the U.S. or return home. Either way, a proverbial ocean of U.S.-educated foreign labor exists. They have the same advanced degrees as U.S. professionals, and they are often willing to work for lower wages.

The Cost of Education in the U.S.

At the same time that the percentage of foreign nationals in our institutions is increasing, our own population is finding it harder to pursue higher education. For example, in the 1970s, the Pell Grant for low-income students could cover up to 40 percent of the average cost of attending a four-year private college. The maximum Pell Grant today only covers approximately 15 percent of the average cost of attending a four-year private college.[23]

According to the NCES, in the 1999–2000 school year about 29 percent of all undergraduates received loans, averaging $5,437. In addition, 44 percent of all undergraduates received grants, averaging $4,949.[24] Compare this with the average cost per year incurred by undergraduates at a four-year private institution, which was $22,520 in the school year 2001–2002.[25]

Let's look at one end of the spectrum. In 2003, the NCES reported that low-income students at private not-for-profit doctoral and liberal arts institutions paid, on average, $9,100 per year.[26] This figure is what a low-income student pays *after* financial aid (grants and loans) has been subtracted from

---

[23] *Richard Kahlenberg, editor,* America's Untapped Resource: Low-Income Students in Higher Education, *(Twentieth Century Fund, 2004)*

[24] *U.S. Department of Education, National Center for Education Statistics,* Digest of Education Statistics *(2002):Table 316, Table 317*

[25] *Ibid.:Table 312*

[26] *Susan P. Choy and Ali M. Berker, "How Families of Low- and Middle-Income Undergraduates Pay for College: Full-Time Dependent Students in 1999–2000,"* Education Statistics Quarterly *5 no. 2 (2003)*

the total cost of attending. Hence, the total cost for an undergraduate degree would be $36,400, not including the loans that must be paid off (easily pushing this number over $40,000).

Now let's look at the other end of the spectrum. For the 2003–2004 academic year, the cost of attending an Ivy League university like Princeton is $39,640 (this includes tuition, room, board, fees, etc.).[27] Thus, completing a B.A. degree at Princeton could cost around $158,560, which is tantamount to buying a house in most parts of the country.[28]

There are those who argue that it's really not that much—that grants, work-study programs, and student loans effectively lower the MSRP of an education like this to an amenable sum of money.

I respectfully disagree with this stance, and now I'll demonstrate why.

Let's assume, for the sake of argument, that after graduating our hypothetical student joins the U.S. Army as an active duty soldier. The Army will cover up to $65,000 on the student loans that our undergraduate has acquired, leaving them in debt for a mere $93,560.

To be generous, let's assume that our Princeton undergraduate held down a part-time job ($1,000 per month) and received grants ($500 per month), after income tax has been taken into account, such that they could cover $12,000 per annum (eight months of school). Over a period of four years, this covers $48,000. Assuming that student loans could cover everything else, this whittles down the total debt to $45,560, which could take around 15 years to pay off.

Even with grants, a part-time job, and enlisting in the Army, our Princeton undergrad will still owe about $45,560. This isn't chump change either; it's serious debt. Those Princeton students who don't enlist in the Army or take a part-time job will be faced with over 30 years worth of debt.

Priced Out of the System

In a 1997 study entitled *Breaking the Social Contract: The Fiscal Crisis in Higher Education*, the Council for Aid to Education (a subsidiary of the RAND think tank) arrived at some rather disturbing conclusions. Specifically, the study determined that "Average real tuition per student, adjusted for inflation, approximately doubled in the 20 years from 1976 to 1995. . . . If it doubles again in the next 20-year period (1996 to 2015), about 6.7 million students will be priced out of the system. In other words, about one out of every two people we would expect to seek a college education will not be able to pay for it. Even if tuition increases by only 25 percent over the 20 years, one out of five students will be excluded."

---

[27] http://www.princeton.edu/pr/facts/profile/03/11.htm

[28] *In the San Francisco Bay Area, this would be a down payment on a house.*

Rising tuition costs are a zero-sum game. Ask yourself one question: cui bono? Who benefits from the rising cost of education and the associated student debt? Who benefits from students having to spend the next decade or two paying off their student loans?

The banks, that's who benefits! Let's look at the Student Loan Corporation as an example. The Student Loan Corporation, an indirect, wholly owned subsidiary of Citigroup, "is one of the nation's leading originators and holders of student loans guaranteed under the Federal Family Education Loan Program, authorized by the Department of Education under the *Federal Higher Education Act of 1965*."[29] In 2002, Student Loan Corporation's annual report indicates that the company generated profits in excess of 175 million. This is almost double the 1999 figure of 89.5 million.

Without a doubt, education in the U.S. is big business. The schools raise tuition, the banks are there to provide the required student loans, and both parties make out just fine. Warren Buffet claims that there's a fool in every market. In this case, the fool in this market is the student. The largest single debt that most people acquire in their lives, aside from buying a house or having children, will be completing a degree.

NOTE Our federal government budgeted $87 billion for the war in Iraq.[30] To get an idea of how much money this is, KeyCorp, Cleveland's largest bank (and the seventeenth largest commercial bank in the U.S.), has net consolidated assets on the order of $84 billion.[31] If our government decided to focus on education the way that it committed itself to Iraq, it could easily offer $40,000 grants to 2,175,000 students (in the 2000–2001 school year, 1,244,171 students earned a bachelor degree[32]). This is enough money to send two waves of undergraduates through school.

Offshoring and Manufacturing

The term *offshoring* is actually short for *offshore outsourcing*. In addition to bringing H-1B and L-1 workers over to the U.S., American corporations have begun to move whole projects, or in some cases entire divisions, overseas to other countries.

This trend first manifested itself in the manufacturing industry, primarily because manufacturing business processes were the easiest to standardize. Corporations moved work overseas to countries where unions had little

---

[29] `http://studentloan.citibank.com/slcsite/fr_about.htm`

[30] *David Firestone and David Stout, "Congress Approves $87 Billion Plan for Iraq and Afghanistan,"* New York Times *(October 17, 2003)*

[31] `http://www.ffiec.gov/nic/`

[32] *U.S. Department of Education, National Center for Education Statistics,* Digest of Education Statistics *(2002): Table 252*

influence, labor laws were lax, and there was a glut of cheaper labor. According to the *Current Employment Statistics* (CES) survey conducted by the U.S. Bureau of Labor Statistics, since 1970 the average annual number of manufacturing jobs has decreased from 17,848,000 to 14,524,000 (see Table 1-4 and Figure 1-2). This represents a net loss of over 3 million jobs, *nearly 19 percent of the 1970 workforce*.

Table 1-4 Decrease in Manufacturing Jobs Since 1970

Year	Workforce (in Thousands)
1970	17,848
1971	17,174
1972	17,669
1973	18,589
1974	18,514
1975	16,909
1976	17,531
1977	18,167
1978	18,932
1979	19,426
1980	18,733
1981	18,634
1982	17,363
1983	17,048
1984	17,920
1985	17,819
1986	17,552
1987	17,609
1988	17,906
1989	17,985
1990	17,695
1991	17,068
1992	16,799
1993	16,774
1994	17,021
1995	17,241
1996	17,237

Year	Workforce (in Thousands)
1997	17,419
1998	17,560
1999	17,322
2000	17,263
2001	16,441
2002	15,306
2003	14,524

Source: Current Employment Statistics *"National Employment, Hours, and Earnings" (Series Id: CEU3000000001)*

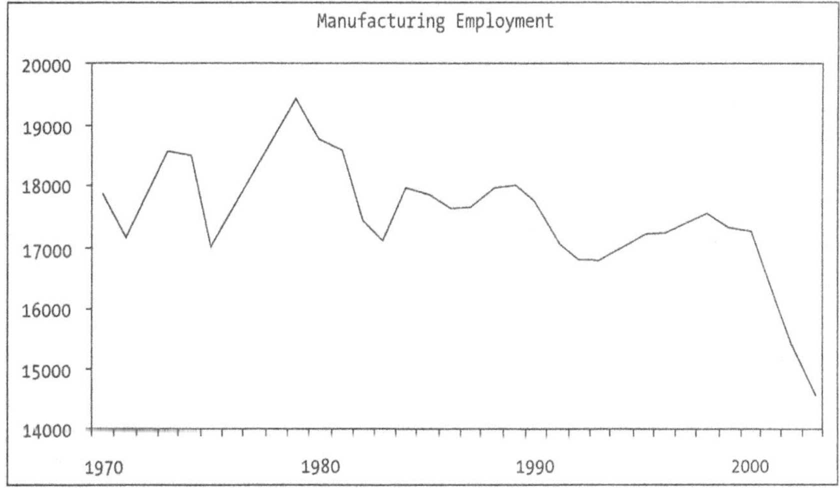

Figure 1-2 Graph of data in Table 1-4

New York City in the 1950s was the vanguard of U.S. manufacturing. Unfortunately, this didn't last very long. The opening of domestic markets via trade agreements, in conjunction with capital flight to foreign countries, transformed New York City into the service-based economy that it is today. New York City, which had approximately a million manufacturing jobs in the 1950s, had only 200,000 by 2001.[33]

By and large, the U.S. economy is now based heavily on the service sector. Table 1-5 breaks down the origins of U.S. Gross Domestic Product (GDP) in 2002. Over three-fourths of the GDP in the U.S. is generated through

[33] *Roger Doyle, "Deindustrialization: Why Manufacturing Continues to Decline,"* Scientific American *(May 4, 2002)*

services.[34] There's no doubt about it, the transformation of the U.S. is complete. This country is no longer the industrial powerhouse that it used to be.

Table 1-5 Origins of GDP in 2002

Sector	Percent of Total GDP
Agriculture	1.4
Manufacturing	21.9
Services	76.7

Some people, from the standpoint of national security, would see this as a long-term strategic error. Ever wondered what would have happened in WWII if we weren't able to mill enough steel to build the tanks that we needed?

The Software Industry Matures

In a sense, the software industry has, until recently, escaped the forces that beset the U.S. manufacturing industry. Up until the mid 1990s, it remained in a suspended state of adolescence. Software companies successfully evaded ancient paradigms like economies of scale and specialization of labor. Most software vendors currently operate like car manufacturers circa 1912 (the year before Henry Ford introduced the assembly line)—they build everything from scratch. They build their own wheels, transmission, and engine. Nothing's interchangeable; each car is unique. It ends up being a huge waste of resources.

The CEO of Oracle, Larry Ellison, believes that the software industry's extended adolescence is coming to an end. Ellison predicts that rising standardization will lead to products that have few, if any, distinguishing features.[35] Companies will rely on mass production to drive down profit margins and put smaller competitors out of business. This will lead to consolidation, as more capable businesses swallow their opponents.

There are those who share Ellison's vision. In November 2002, researchers at Gartner[36] predicted that by the end of 2004, half of the world's software vendors will be acquired or be put out of business. IBM has already embraced the idea of *grid computing*, whereby products are standardized to the extent that they are more like utilities. In October 2002, Sam Palmisano stated that

---

[34] Pocket World in Figures 2003 *(The Economist, 2003)*

[35] *Mylene Mangalindan, "Larry Ellison's Sober Vision,"* Wall Street Journal *(April 8, 2003)*

[36] *Thomas Topolinski and Joanne Correia, "Prediction 2003: Continued Challenges for Software Industry,"* Gartner Research *AV-18-8042 (November 20, 2002)*

IBM would be committing $10 billion towards *on-demand computing*, which aims to turn software services into a commodity.[37]

Then there's the last piece of the puzzle: job exports. Like the manufacturing industry, which relocated facilities in an effort to minimize cost structure, the software industry will move development outside the U.S. in the search for lower-cost labor.

Third-World Development

The ability of corporations to utilize offshore outsourcing is a result of several economic and technical developments working in conjunction. Specifically, I'm talking about foreign countries

- Investing in their educational system
- Constructing high-speed data networks
- Leveraging network-enabled collaboration tools
- Employing modern software technology

Let's look at India as an example.

India has taken steps to develop its own educational system. According to India's Department of Education, India currently has over 12,000 institutions of higher learning and employs 331,000 teachers to instruct over 7 million students. Compare this to U.S. figures from the 2002 *Digest of Educational Statistics*. In 2002, the U.S. had over 4,000 colleges and universities, manned by over a million faculty members. Over 15 million students attended U.S. institutions of higher learning during the 2000–2001 school year.[38] Thus, while India doesn't have the sheer scale of the U.S. system, it's making headway.

The key to accessing India's mass of IT workers has been the construction of a high-bandwidth networking infrastructure. India's Department of Information Technology states that India has installed satellite earth stations that communicate with the Intelsat system. They exist in places like Bangalore, Hyderabad, Thiruvananthapuram, Gandhinagar, Noida, and Bhubaneswar. These type F-3, wide-band installations serve as the country's international gateways to the global communication system and are the foundation of the country's ability to offshore.

The emergence of network-based collaborative technology allows American multinationals to interact easily with their offshore divisions. If face-to-face, real-time meetings are required, video-conferencing can be utilized.

---

[37] *Ludwig Siegele, "At Your Service: Despite Early Failures, Computing Will Eventually Become a Utility,"* The Economist *(May 16, 2003)*

[38] *U.S. Department of Education, National Center for Education Statistics,* Digest of Education Statistics *(2002): Table 170*

If face-to-face isn't an issue, then conference calls will fit the bill. If the cost of a dedicated phone line is an issue, voice-over-IP technology can be used to make a calling center more affordable.

Other tools like e-mail and instant messaging programs can also be used to communicate. Source code versioning tools like GNU's CVS package or Perforce's SCM suite allow a geo-distributed team of engineers to concurrently work together on a common repository of source code.

Finally, the evolution of modular software technology has also facilitated offshoring of programming work. Object-oriented programming languages like C++ and Java allow the constituents of a program to be broken down into stand-alone components. The inventors of C++ (Bjarne Stroustrup) and Java (James Gosling) originally created their languages specifically to be used in the implementation of large-scale software projects.

The idea behind these languages is that the various parts of a program could be constructed from components, the software equivalent of LEGOs. A group of engineers could divide up into small teams and build their own set of LEGO-like components. When they were done, the engineers collect their components and integrate them together into a LEGO gestalt. If changes needed to be made, the engineers would be able to swap components in and out easily, just like LEGO pieces.

Object-oriented languages like Java and C++ basically assist in the division of labor. In terms of offshoring, this means that a software architect can now write up specs for software components and ship them off to be implemented by offshore workers.

The Bottom Line ($$$)

The fundamental motivation for offshoring is cost savings. Public relations consultants can dress offshore outsourcing up any way they want to, but they can't hide the truth. It is a well-known fact that the GDP in countries like China and India is a fraction of that in the U.S. Table 1-6 displays the GDP per capita, in U.S. dollars, for the United States and other potential sources of offshore labor. I have ordered Table 1-6 from high to low to give you a feel for where different countries lie on the spectrum.

Table 1-6 GDP per Capita

Country	GDP per Capita (2002 USD)
USA	$36,300
Ireland	$29,300
Singapore	$25,200
Israel	$19,500

Country	GDP per Capita (2002 USD)
Russia	$9,700
Mexico	$8,900
China	$4,700
India	$2,600

Source: CIA, World Fact Book

According to the U.S. Bureau of Labor Statistics (*2002 National Occupational Employment and Wage Estimates*), the average salary of a software engineer in the U.S. is $73,800 (see Table 1-7).

Table 1-7 IT Salaries

SOC	Title	Number Employed in 2002	Mean Annual Pay
15-1011	Information Scientists	24,410	$80,510
15-1021	Computer Programmers	457,320	$63,690
15-1031	Software Engineer	356,760	$73,800
15-1041	Support Specialists	478,560	$42,320
15-1051	Computer Systems Analysts	467,750	$64,890
15-1061	Database Administrators	102,090	$59,080
15-1071	Systems Administrators	232,560	$57,620
15-1081	Communications Analysts	133,460	$61,390
15-2011	Actuaries	14,440	$80,780
15-2021	Mathematicians	2,600	$75,610
15-2031	Operations Research Analysts	56,310	$60,890
15-2041	Statisticians	17,820	$60,000
15-2091	Mathematical Technicians	1,970	$42,920
15-0000	Totals	2,772,620	$61,630

NOTE In Table 1-7, SOC stands for *Standard Occupational Classification.* The government thrives on acronyms.

Compare the average salary for all IT professionals in Table 1-7 (i.e., $61,630) with those of their international counterparts in Table 1-8.

Table 1-8 Foreign IT Salaries

Country	Average Salary
USA	$61,630
Singapore	$33,504
Ireland	$23,000–$34,000
Israel	$15,000–$38,000
China	$8,952
India	$5,880–$11,000
Russia	$5,000–$7,500
Mexico	$1,400

Source: Stephanie Overby, "A Buyer's Guide to Offshore Outsourcing," CIO Magazine *(November 15, 2002)*

Now the motivation behind offshoring should be clear. There are roughly 2.7 million American software employees in the U.S. making on average $61,630. Why would you pay an American $61,630 a year when you can get a U.S.-trained worker in India for a percentage of this amount? A crackerjack engineering graduate from the Indian Institute of Technology (IITS) can demand a salary of up to $10,000.[39] That's one sixth of the U.S. average!

IBM, on behalf of its own internal accounting process, has calculated that a software engineer in China with three to five years of experience costs $12.50 an hour, compared to an equivalent American engineer, who costs $56 an hour.[40] A programmer in China costs less than a fourth of their American counterparts!

Q.E.D.

[39] *Manjeet Kripalani and Pete Engardio, "The Rise of India,"* Business Week *(December 8, 2003)*

[40] *William M. Bulkeley, "IBM Data Give Rare Look at Sensitive 'Offshoring' Plans,"* Dow Jones Business News *(January 19, 2004)*

CHAPTER 2

Measuring the Trend

Chapter at a Glance

All I know is what I read in the papers.
—Will Rogers

In the previous chapter, I looked at forces that gave rise to offshoring and the immediate financial motivations behind its increasing popularity. In this chapter, I look at who's offshoring and what the experts think about its possible future implications.

Scarcity of Data

If you can formulate a metric for a process, you can collect measurements. If you can collect measurements, then you can perform an analysis. The final step is to take your analysis and use it to construct a forecast.

One of the problems associated with analyzing offshore outsourcing is that companies have been fairly tight-lipped about it—which is to say that data on outsourcing is difficult to acquire. The Bureau of Labor Statistics (BLS) doesn't include offshoring as a factor in its calculations. The U.S. Department of Commerce doesn't collect offshoring numbers, nor does the Bureau of U.S. Citizenship and Immigration.

When I was a graduate student, I took a course in mathematical statistics taught by Peter Ritchken. He warned us that "if you don't have much data, that's when you should start to get scared." Now, I don't have enough data to make a quantitative prediction. However, I believe that I have enough data to verify that a trend exists and that it's significant.

To gather data, I scavenged through newspaper articles and called up companies directly. None of the corporations returned my calls (big surprise). The minute that they found out who I was and what I was doing, they cut off contact. The multinationals know that broaching the topic of offshoring has the potential to create a nasty backlash. "The problem is that companies aren't sure if it's politically correct to talk about it," claims Jack Trout, president of Trout & Partners. "Nobody has come up with a way to spin it in a positive way."[1]

NOTE It's rumored that Microsoft, in attempt to keep things quiet, has gone so far as to remove its name from the minibuses that it uses to ferry around engineers in India.[2]

When I worked for Lawson Software in Minnesota, managers once tried referring to cubes as "workstations" in a ridiculous attempt to avoid negative connotations. Likewise, large American corporations have begun to try and

[1] *David Zielenziger, "U.S. Companies Moving More Jobs Overseas,"* Reuters *(December 23, 2003)*

[2] *Ibid.*

rename offshore outsourcing in an attempt to hide the awful truth. Synonyms for *offshoring* include *sourcing*, *offshore partnerships*, and *multishoring*.

Like the bootleggers who traveled under cover of darkness, large transnational corporations are hoping that they can quietly move jobs overseas without drawing too much attention to themselves. Otherwise, American workers might realize the true extent of what's going on and do something to retaliate, like implementing a product boycott, or forming a union, or getting politically active.

What's Going Offshore?

The types of service-based jobs going offshore can be broken down into four tiers (see Figure 2-1). The lowest tier consists of back-office duties (a.k.a. *operations*) that can be standardized almost to the extent of factory work. *Customer contact* is the next tier up; it requires a slightly more sophisticated labor force due to the added ingredient of communication.

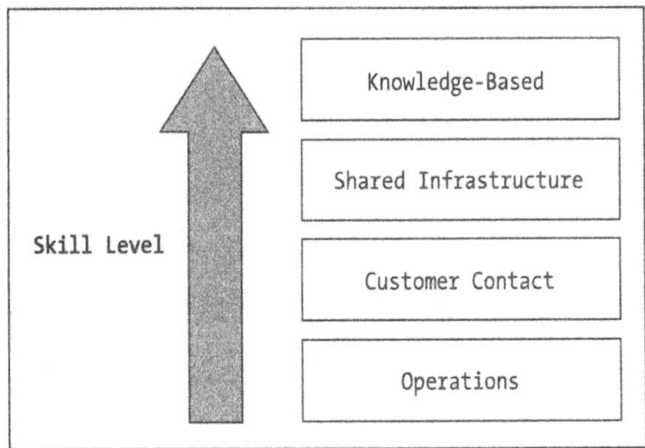

Figure 2-1 Skill set requirements for different tasks

Above customer contact is the *infrastructure* tier, consisting of skilled tasks that most companies have to execute. Infrastructure jobs typically require a bachelor degree or a two-year associates degree. Many companies have taken redundant geo-distributed services, like accounting and IT, and centralized them in one location overseas.

At the top level are the *knowledge-based* positions, which typically require an advanced degree (a master's degree or Ph.D.). These are highly skilled, high-paying jobs that require a significant amount of training.

Both operations and customer contact work are essentially *rules-based*. Tasks are defined in terms of specific guidelines, such that they can be treated like commodities. Infrastructure and knowledge-based jobs are *judgment-based*. They require an employee to adapt to different situations and solve new problems.

The following four lists should provide you with a basic idea of the types of jobs that exist in each tier.

Rules-Based Work

Operations	Customer Contact

Transaction processing
  Insurance claims
  Loans
  Credit Cards
	Inbound call center

Data entry	Outbound call center
Medical transcription	Telemarketing
Document management	Customer surveys
	Collections
	Internet-based support
	Answering e-mails
	User Forums

Judgment-Based Work

Shared Infrastructure	Knowledge-Based
Finance and accounting	Content development and design

Information technology
  Help desk
  System administration
  Software testing
  Software maintenance
  Software development
	Software architecture

Disaster recovery
  Redundant systems
  Daily backups
	Risk assessment, analysis (e.g., actuarial)

	Product design

	Research and development (R&D)
	  Software
	  Semiconductor
	  Aerospace
	  Securities
	  Pharmaceutical

According to the National Association for Software Service Companies (NASSCOM), business process outsourcing services enabled by information technology (ITES-BPO) accounts for almost 25 percent of India's 2002 software and services revenue. In 2002, ITES-BPO–related work in India experienced a growth of 59 percent and generated $2.3 billion. Table 2-1 breaks down this number by service.

Table 2-1 Services Outsourced to India

Service	Employment	Revenue (in Millions)
Customer care	65,000	810
Finance	24,000	510
HR	2,100	45
Payment service	11,000	210
Administration	25,000	310
Content development	44,000	465
Total	**171,100**	**2350**

Source: NASSCOM ITES BPO FAQ (`http://www.nascom.org`)

Most of the articles and studies that I have read seem to agree implicitly that some jobs are easier to offshore than others. According to Cynthia Kroll, jobs sent offshore have the following attributes:[3]

- No face-to-face customer service requirements
- High-information content
- Network-enabled work process
- High wage differential with occupations in destination country
- Low setup barrier
- Low social networking requirement

This covers a lot of ground. In fact, some people would argue that corporations will offshore anything that doesn't require direct face-to-face contact. According to Thea Lee, the chief international economist for the AFL-CIO, "Anything that isn't nailed to the floor is being considered for outsourcing."[4]

[3] *Ashok Deo Bardhan and Cynthia Kroll, "The New Wave of Outsourcing" (Fisher Center for Real Estate and Urban Economics, U.C. Berkeley, November 2, 2003)*

[4] *Bob Herbert, "Bracing for the Blow,"* New York Times *(December 26, 2003)*

Safe Havens

You might be wondering to yourself, are there any service-based jobs that are safe from being sent offshore? Such jobs would have attributes that are the inverse of those in Kroll's list. For example:

- Face-to-face customer service requirements
- Work process that can't be network-enabled
- Low wage differential with occupations in destination country
- High setup barrier
- High social networking requirement

In my opinion, the key element is the face-to-face element. Any job that requires you to physically be here in the U.S. is safe from offshoring over the long run. Of course, this does nothing to protect you from H-1B and L-1 visa holders. The following list offers a set of industry domains that I view as being resistant to offshore outsourcing.

Offshore-Resistant Fields:

Healthcare
  Doctors
  Nurses
Real estate
Construction
Maintenance
Law
Marketing and advertising
High-level sales, Pre-sales
Software installation
Government
  Department of Defense
  Department of Homeland Security
  Department of Justice

The baby boomers are getting older. As this happens, there will be a boom in healthcare. The need for face-to-face doctor-patient interaction will offer a degree of security to medical professionals, although routine medical work, in some cases, has already been outsourced. For example, Massachusetts General Hospital, in Boston, contracts Indian radiologists to process x-ray images.[5]

The legal profession requires practicing attorneys to pass a bar exam and be familiar with local and state legislation. These constraints can present a

[5] *Marla Dickerson, "Offshoring Trend Casting a Wider Net,"* Los Angeles Times *(January 4, 2004)*

formidable barrier to entry. Court trials also require lawyers to appear in person, which could present considerable travel expenses to someone living in another country.

There are a couple of other jobs, like marketing and government work, that don't necessarily require you to be in the U.S. However, I still think they are safe jobs. For example, successful marketing often depends so heavily on subtle behavioral factors (e.g., societal mores, pop-culture references) that I don't think it could be sent over to India or China. Working for a military or for a federal agency is also safe because they require citizenship and a security clearance.

Short-Term Advice for Software Developers

As software development fades away as a viable career path, one short-term survival strategy would be to move into areas like contract management and requirements analysis, which demand a higher-level skill set.

Requirement analysis consists of working with a project's customer to determine what the finished product should do (i.e., what is this program *required* to do?). The resulting guidelines must be specific enough to allow the software engineers to implement the project, but at the same time focus must be kept on the end user so that customers get what they asked for.

With regard to offshoring, American engineers could reposition themselves as requirements analysts. The face-to-face nature of this work with customers is the key. American engineers can leverage their connection to existing customers, and then pass off requirements to their counterparts overseas.

With a growing demand for offshore labor, there's probably a dearth of people who have experience in establishing and overseeing relationships with offshore service providers. This is one reason why contract management is a good contingency. A contract manager is responsible for developing an operational plan with offshore providers. This arrangement defines mission goals, budget parameters, and performance metrics. The contract manager then optimizes return on investment through performance-based contracting.[6]

NOTE Of course, there's nothing to prevent companies from offshoring or outsourcing contract management and requirements analysis later on, which is why I call them *short-term* strategies. Another problem with this train of thought is that most companies only have one or two high-level design architects. It's unreasonable to expect all of the displaced software engineers to be able to find this type of work.

[6] *Joe Santana, "Two Steps to Protecting Your Job from Offshore Outsourcing,"* TechRepublic.com *(October 16, 2003,* `http://techrepublic.com.com/5100-6316_11-5074311.html`*)*

Who's Going Offshore?

The following survey looks at which corporations are offshoring. I stuck to large Fortune 100 organizations primarily because I think that they will set the bar for everyone else. Their success with offshoring, or lack thereof, will decide the future of offshoring as a cost-saving strategy.

High-Tech

High-tech work (software engineering, program maintenance, R&D) often involves a great deal of thinking, an activity that can be done anywhere. This is one reason why many of the really large-scale offshore outsourcing projects have been undertaken in the software and hardware industries. Take a look at Table 2-2. Four of the top five employers in India are high-tech companies.[7]

Table 2-2 Top Five Employers in India

Company	Indian Employees
General Electric	17,800 employees
Hewlett-Packard	11,000 employees
IBM	6,000 employees
American Express	4,000 employees
Dell	3,800 employees

Source: Wired *magazine*

Of all the companies that I examined, high-tech companies offered the most concrete information on offshore outsourcing. This is because when they initially started doing it, they incorrectly assumed that it would boost their stock value. They blithely concluded that it would make them seem more efficient relative to their competitors.

High-tech corporations weren't expecting resistance. Maybe they assumed that laid-off American employees, like Mike Emmons, wouldn't be vocal. In the wake of a rising backlash, everyone has become *very* quiet. Unfortunately, it's too late to take back all of their original announcements.

Table 2-3, courtesy of Morgan Stanley India,[8] should offer you a preliminary look at who's in India and what their plans are. Although I think I should add that some of the numbers that you see in Table 2-3 might not exactly agree with what you read later on.

---

[7] *Daniel H. Pink, "The New Face ofThe Silicon Age,"* Wired *(February, 2004)*

[8] *Stephen Roach, "The Global Labor Arbitrage,"* Morgan Stanley Global Economic Forum *(October 6, 2003)*

Table 2-3 American Companies' Plans for India

Company	Latest Manpower	India Manpower	Plans for India Office
Accenture	65,000	3,500	8,000 employees by August 2004
Adobe Systems	3,250	185	250 people in six months
Cadence	5,000	315	Doubling team in four years
Cisco	34,466	2,300	NA
EDS	138,000	300	2,400 people by 2005
i2	2,800	1,000	Recruiting actively
IBM	150,000	3,100	10,000 people in three years
Intel	79,200	950	3,000 people by 2005
Lucent	35,000	570	NA
Microsoft	55,000	200	500 people in three years
Oracle	40000	3,159	6,000 people in the next 12 months
Sun Microsystems	36,000	700	Growing the India Center
Texas Instruments	34,400	900	1,500 people by March 2006
Xansa	5,583	1,200	6,000 people in a few years

Source: Morgan Stanley India

IBM

In 2002, International Business Machine, a.k.a. Big Blue, had 145,705 employees in the U.S. and 315,889 worldwide. For the nine-month period ending in September 2003, IBM's total revenue was $63.2 billion. IBM is so big that it's literally a world unto itself. In fact, it's so large that sometimes it takes a while for news from the outside to make its way in. An IBM engineer once told me, "Inside IBM, OS/2 is still seen as a viable desktop operating system." He said that with a straight face.

In the summer of 2003, IBM employed 5,400 workers in India.[9] According to *Wired* magazine, this number has grown to 6,000. In December 2003, someone on the inside leaked internal documents to the *Wall Street Journal* that detailed plans to move 4,700 jobs offshore;[10] *Merry Christmas, you're fired*. Of course, IBM spokesman James Sciales declined to comment on this.

[9] *Eric Auchard, "One in 10 U.S. Tech Jobs May Move Overseas, Report Says,"* Reuters *(July 29, 2003)*

[10] *"IBM to Move Software Jobs to India, China,"* Associated Press *(December 17, 2003)*

IBM, which has been in India since 1951, plans to boost its staff there to 10,000 by 2005.[11]

In January 2004, an IBM spokesman stated that the company planned to shift 3,000 jobs to India over the course of the year.[12] The spokesman also mentioned that IBM plans to hire 15,000 employees total in 2004, 10,000 of which will be outside of the U.S.[13]

Microsoft

Microsoft currently has 54,468 employees worldwide. In 2003, Microsoft accumulated total revenue to the tune of $32.3 billion. In November 2002, Bill Gates announced that over the next three years, Microsoft would be spending $400 million dollars to build up its presence in India. He also stated that Microsoft would also be investing $750 million in China for R&D and outsourcing.[14] Microsoft is moving over a billion dollars worth of capital offshore.

Who's behind this move? Bill Gates KBE, Knight Commander of the British Empire.[15]

People who think that the U.S. has a stranglehold on innovation would be well advised to visit Microsoft's Beijing R&D laboratory, where one third of the 180 researchers have Ph.D.s from American universities (remember from Chapter 1, roughly 40 to 50 percent of American Ph.D.s in the hard sciences are held by foreign nationals). This group had a role in implementing the "digital ink" technology that Microsoft's Tablet PCs use to process human handwriting.[16]

In 2003, Microsoft announced that it would add 4,000 positions here in the U.S. and 1,000 overseas.[17] By 2005, Microsoft plans to triple the size of its Hyderabad operation to 500.[18]

Intel

Intel currently has 78,000 employees worldwide. For the nine-month period ending in September 2003, Intel's total revenue was $21.4 billion.

---

[11] *Jed Graham, "Tech Layoffs Fading, But No Hiring Boom,"* Investor's Business Daily *(October 20, 2003)*

[12] *William M. Bulkeley, "IBM Data Give Rare Look at Sensitive 'Offshoring' Plans,"* Dow Jones Business News *(January 19, 2003)*

[13] *Ibid.*

[14] *Pete Engardio, Aaron Bernstein, and Manjeet Kripalani, "The New Global Job Shift,"* BusinessWeek *(February 3, 2003)*

[15] *"Bill Gates to Receive Honorary Knighthood,"* Associated Press *(January 25, 2003)*

[16] *Ibid.*

[17] *Kristi Heim, "Labor Group Protests Offshore Tech Hiring,"* Mercury News *(January 5, 2003)*

[18] *Steve Lohr, "Offshoring: Opportunity or Threat,"* New York Times *(December 23, 2003)*

Intel's offshoring policy is schizophrenic in nature. On one hand, Intel is actively sending jobs overseas. On the other hand, Andy Grove has warned congress that "When the problem becomes obvious, it will be too late—and the outcome will be too depressing, even for me."[19] It reminds me of an obese person telling Jerry Springer he just can't help himself. "I'd like to stop, Jerry, but I can't. Boo-hoo-hoo!"

Intel has 60 percent of its labor force in the U.S., but over the years it has moved 1,000 jobs offshore to India and China to decrease cost structure.[20] By the end of 2005, Intel plans to have 3,000 employees in India.

Again, for those who don't think that creative, innovative work isn't going offshore: Intel's Bangalore campus defines the cutting edge for R&D on the company's 32-bit processors for wireless products and servers. According to Intel India's president, Ketan Sampat, "These are corporate crown jewels."[21]

Oracle

As of May 31, 2003, Oracle had 40,650 employees worldwide and had earned total revenue of $9.5 billion.

During the peak of England's colonial era, people would say, "The sun never sets on the British empire." In this spirit, Larry Ellison is hoping to establish redundant facilities around the world to support 24-hour software development and other services, such that the sun never sets on Ellison's empire.

Anyone who's ever visited Oracle's headquarters in Redwood City (all 2.5 million square feet of it) knows why it's called the "Emerald City." The industrial park is dominated by a number of tall green office towers. Oracle is hoping to replicate this with an "Emerald India." Oracle's plans to employ 6,000 Indian workers at its seven-acre Hyderabad campus (15 percent of its current workforce), doubling its head count. In keeping with this goal, by the end of 2004, Oracle plans to expand its Indian workforce from 3,000 to 4,000.[22]

Oracle formed its Indian subsidiary, Oracle India, back in 1993. In 1996, Oracle India was given three months to develop a new product from the ground up. The Indian engineers worked around the clock, easily beating code cutoff deadlines. Within three months, the Indian engineers delivered the product's second-generation implementation. This accomplishment turned Oracle India from an engineering backwater into one of the company's strategic assets.[23] Again, for those who think that the U.S. has a monopoly on design and innovation . . .

---

[19] *Lisa DiCarlo, "Intel Chief: U.S. Losing Tech Lead, Jobs,"* Forbes.com *(October 10, 2003)*

[20] *Mark Larson, "Oracle Sends Its Rocklin Jobs to India,"* Sacramento Business Journal *(October 13, 2003)*

[21] *Manjeet Kripalani and Pete Engardio, "The Rise of India,"* BusinessWeek *(December 8, 2003)*

[22] *Aaron Davis, "Software Developers Calling Shots,"* Mercury News *(November 9, 2003)*

[23] *Ibid.*

HP

There is no job that is America's God-given right anymore.
—Carly Fiorina, chief executive

Worldwide, Hewlett-Packard has 141,800 employees. As of the business year ending on October 31, 2003, the company's total revenue was $73.1 billion. According to a *CNETAsia* article in December 2003, HP has the distinction of being one of the largest transnational IT employers in India. HP currently employs 10,000 Indian workers (roughly 7 percent of the total HP workforce).[24] This figure differs from *Wired* magazine's figure of 11,000.

It seems like Ms. Fiorina practices what she preaches.

HP employs 6,000 workers in Singapore.[25] On Tuesday, January 13, 2003, HP announced that it would be investing a billion dollars in Singapore to bolster its manufacturing base there.[26]

HP will also be investing $55 million over the next three years to establish an R&D facility in Singapore to work on networking hardware. HP had an existing facility in Roseville, California, *but the company claimed it had a hard time finding engineering talent to fill positions.*[27] According to Vice President John McHugh:

> *We looked at our ability to recruit skilled engineers in Sacramento and the Bay Area and it became clear we needed to tap into a broader workforce . . . to free up our U.S. resources for the areas of network security and wireless networking.*

I wonder if Ms. Fiorina is going to outsource her entourage of beauticians?

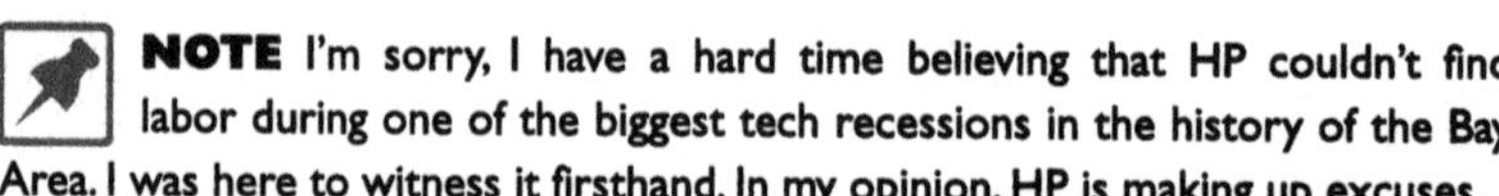

NOTE I'm sorry, I have a hard time believing that HP couldn't find labor during one of the biggest tech recessions in the history of the Bay Area. I was here to witness it firsthand. In my opinion, HP is making up excuses.

GE

General Electric employs over 315,000 people worldwide. GE's 2002 total revenue topped out at $131.7 billion. GE has a presence in over 100 countries. In India alone, GE has 17,800 employees (about 6 percent of the total).[28]

I've said it before, and I'll say it again: offshoring innovation and creative work is more common than the critics contend. GE's John Welch Technology

---

[24] *"HP Marks Indian Employment Milestone,"* CNETAsia *(December 4, 2003)*

[25] *"HP to Invest $1 Billion in Singapore,"* Reuters *(January 13, 2003)*

[26] *Ibid.*

[27] *Bryan Lee, "HP Bases New Research Centre in Singapore,"* The Straits Times *(August 1, 2003)*

[28] *Daniel H. Pink, "The New Face of the Silicon Age,"* Wired *(February, 2004)*

Center in India employs 1,800 engineers (450 of which have Ph.D.s). Since 2000, the center has filed for 95 patents. Says Director Guillerno Wille, "The game here really isn't about saving costs, but to speed innovation and generate growth for the company."[29]

Dell

Dell Inc., the leading vendor of personal computers, employs 44,300 people worldwide. During the nine months ending on October 31, 2003, Dell generated a total revenue of $29.9 billion.

Approximately 32 percent of Dell's employees are outside of the U.S. In India alone, Dell employs over 2,000 workers[30] (*Wired* puts the total at 3,800). During the recent recession, Dell laid off 5,700 workers (most of them call center staff in Texas). In the third quarter of 2003, over half of the 2,500 jobs added were overseas.[31] Dell attributes this to growth in international sales.

In November 2003, customer complaints prompted Dell to move call center jobs back to the U.S. from India.[32] Dell wouldn't indicate how many, and indicated that its commitment to India was still very strong. Perhaps Dell's Indian employees need to work on their Texas twang.

Motorola

Motorola employs approximately 97,000 people. The company's revenue for the first nine months ending in September 2003 was $19 billion.

Not much of Motorola is left in the U.S. The company spent $1 billion moving production to China and another $90 million moving R&D to China.[33] Motorola employs over 12,000 people in China. The company's 2002 investment in China was $3.4 billion.[34] Let's break down the employment figure a little. Motorola's manufacturing center in Tianjin is the company's largest. It employs over 10,000 workers. Motorola's PCS China operation employs over 4,000 people.

According to Motorola,[35] the company has 16 R&D centers in China, employing over 1,300 R&D engineers. Motorola expects to increase this number to 4,000 by 2006, in addition to spending $1.3 billion on R&D. Once more, this illustrates the migration of knowledge-based work offshore.

---

[29] *Manjeet Kripalani and Pete Engardio, "The Rise of India,"* BusinessWeek *(December 8, 2003)*

[30] *"Offshoring: Lost in Translation,"* The Economist *(November 27, 2003)*

[31] *Amy Schatz, "Dell Sending Some Jobs Back to US,"* Austin American Statesman *(November 21, 2003)*

[32] *Ibid.*

[33] *Diane Alden, "America Unmade,"* NewsMax.com *(May 22, 2003,* `http://www.newsmax.com/archives/articles/2003/5/22/15302.shtml`*)*

[34] `http://www.motorola.com.cn/en/about/inchina/china.asp`

[35] `http://www.motorola.com.cn/en/about/inchina/joint.asp`

Finance

Large banks have been offshore outsourcing also; it's just that they haven't been as brazen about it as the high-tech companies. Financial institutions like Citigroup and Bank of America quietly moved back office and call center jobs offshore. Once this proved viable, some institutions have also sent higher-level analysis work offshore.

Unlike the high-tech corporations, the banks didn't really brag about their offshoring capabilities, so the data I have on bank offshoring isn't as extensive.

Before I jump into the banks, I want to show you an interesting bit of data from our friends at the U.S. Federal Reserve. According to the Federal Reserve's National Information Center,[36] the top five largest banks in the U.S. are as listed in Table 2-4.

Table 2-4 Top U.S. Banks

Bank	Net Consolidated Assets
Citigroup	1,208,923,000,000
J.P. Morgan Chase & Co.	792,700,000,000
Bank of America Corporation	736,935,000,000
Wells Fargo & Company	390,813,000,000
Wachovia Corporation	388,767,000,000

Source: Federal Reserve, National Information Center

Naturally, I'm going to look at the top three. I'm also going to examine Merrill Lynch and Lehman Brothers.

Citigroup

Citigroup has 275,000 employees in over 100 countries. Citigroup's India office was opened in 1902. Citigroup India employs 5,000 people.

According to a joint study done by McKinsey and EDS, Citigroup has sent approximately 1,100 jobs offshore, achieving a cost savings of 50 percent.[37] These jobs had to do with card processing, retail account maintenance, trade finance, and cash management.

Not only does Citigroup send labor offshore, but the company also has ownership in an offshore service provider. In April of 2002, Infosys announced that Citigroup would be making a $20 million dollar investment in Progeon, an IT Business Process Outsourcing (BPO) provider.

---

[36] `http://www.ffiec.gov/nic/`

[37] *Vinay Kumar and Gabe David, "Offshore Services—Maximizing the Benefits for Financial Institutes,"* Journal of Financial Transformation *no. 8 (Capco Institute, 2003)*

Who Controls the Fed?

A plethora of conspiracy theories floating around the Internet claim that the Federal Reserve is secretly controlled by a small group of international bankers (e.g., the Warburg Interests, the Schiff interests, House of Rothschild, the Lloyds of London). In the mid 1990s, WRUW in Cleveland aired a lengthy program that railed against the U.S. Centralize Banking system (i.e., paper money isn't constitutional). My own feelings of doubt led me to query Dr. Joe Haubrich, an economics researcher at the Cleveland Federal Reserve.

Granted, the Federal Reserve isn't a federal body. It's a private institution that is owned by its member banks.[38] The government only has influence insofar as the U.S. president appoints the seven governors of the Federal Reserve Board (for 14-year terms). These seven governors control 7 of the 12 voting chairs in the *Federal Open Market Committee* (FOMC). The presidents of the 12 Federal Reserve District Banks control the remaining 5 chairs. Each district's board of directors elects these presidents, such that they represent the interests of the member banks, and not the general public. This is how the member banks exert control.

Thus, to find out who has influence with the Federal Reserve, you will have to determine who owns the member banks. Answering this question will tell you how much authority foreign interests garner. I don't want to ruin the fun for you—think of it as an extended homework assignment.

J.P. Morgan Chase

J.P. Morgan Chase employs 94,335 people worldwide. For the first nine months of 2003, the company generated a net income of about $4.9 billion.

In December 2002, J.P. Morgan Chase signed a $5 billion seven-year outsourcing deal with IBM. In a deal affecting 4,000 IT staff members, IBM agreed to maintain the bank's voice and data networks, in addition to offering help desk services.[39] There was no indication whether offshore labor would be utilized.

In a move that demonstrates the vulnerability of knowledge-based jobs, J.P. Morgan Chase has recently taken on 1,000 employees in Bombay to augment its equity research department.[40]

---

[38] *William Greider,* Secrets of the Temple *(Simon and Schuster, 1987)*

[39] *Paul Mcdougall, "J.P. Morgan Chase Signs $5B Services Deal,"* InformationWeek *(December 30, 2003,* `http://www.informationweek.com/story/IWK20021230S0001`*)*

[40] *William Sherman, "City Tech Jobs Down Drain,"* New York Daily News *(June 1, 2003)*

Bank of America

Bank of America employs 133,549 people full time. In 2003, the company's net income was $10.8 billion.

In 2002, Bank of America laid off 3,700 of its technical and back-office workers, about 15 percent of all such jobs in the company (25,000). In 2003, 1,100 jobs were sent to India.[41] In 2004, Bank of America will take things a step further by establishing a new subsidiary in India.[42]

American Express

American Express employs over 75,000 people worldwide. In 2002, the company's total revenue was $23.8 billion.

In a 2002 outsourcing deal reputed to be worth over $4 billion, and which affected over 6,000 workers, American Express relegated the core of its IT operations infrastructure over to IBM Global Services.[43] Some of the 2,000 American Express employees who transferred to IBM were laid off during the market downturn, but neither party would mention how many.

According to *Wired*, American express employs 4,000 over in India. The company used Indian programmers to develop software that reconciles customer accounts. This software now reconciles more than 500,000 accounts daily, over 75 percent of the total. American Express paid $5,000 to engineer the solution and calculates that an equivalent commercial solution would have cost several million dollars in licensing fees.[44]

Merrill Lynch

Merrill Lynch employs 47,800 people worldwide. As of the third quarter of 2003, the company generated total revenue of $15.2 billion.

In the fall of 2003, Merrill Lynch started to roll out a new desktop platform for its financial analysts. Merrill Lynch outsourced the entire project to Thomson Financial in a five-year deal worth $1 billion.[45] Thomson serves as a general contractor, subcontracting labor to other companies like Ernst & Young, HP, IBM, and Microsoft. The project's goal is to provide Merrill's 14,000 financial analysts with new workstations and more powerful software.

---

[41] *Pete Engardio, Aaron Bernstein, and Manjeet Kripalani, "The New Global Job Shift,"* BusinessWeek *(February 3, 2003,* `http://www.businessweek.com/magazine/content/03_05/b3818001.htm`*)*

[42] *"Bank of America to Boost Outsourcing to India,"* Reuters *(October 14, 2003)*

[43] *Todd R. Weiss, "American Express Signs $4B IT Services Deal with IBM,"* Computerworld *(March 4, 2002,* `http://www.computerworld.com/industrytopics/financial/story/0,10801,68729,00.html`*)*

[44] *Vivek Agrawal, Diana Farrell, and Jaana K. Remes, "Offshoring and Beyond,"* The McKinsey Quarterly, Global Directions *no. 4 (2003)*

[45] *Todd Datz, "Merrill Lynch's Billion Dollar Bet,"* CIO Magazine *(September 15, 2003)*

While the company's outsourcing has been aggressive, less is known of the company's movement towards offshore employment. According to spokeswoman Selena Morris, "We have 10,000 tech workers and less than 1,000 of them, around 800, are overseas."[46]

Lehman Brothers

Lehman Brothers employs 12,300 people worldwide. It's noteworthy as an example because, like Dell, Lehman decided to bring back help desk support to the U.S. from India. Lehman cited the need to offer help desk services in real time.[47]

Of the 450 staff that Lehman has in India, slightly over 20 positions will be displaced. Lehman stated that this has not changed its commitment to India and that its presence there will increase as a whole. According to Charlie Cortese, managing director of IT, "We are happy with our relationship with Wipro; our work with them is going up."[48]

Insurance

Insurance can almost be thought of as a branch in the finance tree. Like other financial institutions, insurance companies deal in risk (e.g., quantifying, assessing, and predicting). Like the banks, insurance companies have been very quiet about their offshore activities. Routine work, like document management, wasn't the only thing that insurance companies sent overseas.

MetLife

MetLife employs 48,500 people worldwide. MetLife's net income for the nine-month period ending on September 30, 2003, was $1.5 billion.

MetLife has used an offshore service provider named Cognizant Technology Solutions Corp. to manage its human resource systems from remote Indian data centers. MetLife claims that sending the work offshore has resulted in savings on the order of 30 percent. Cognizant has 350 of its employees working on the project.[49]

Business has been good for Cognizant. At the end of 2003, Cognizant had approximately 9,000 employees. The company plans to expand its headcount to 13,000 in 2004.[50] Cognizant has offices in Calcutta, Hyderabad, Bangalore, Pune, and Chennai. About 7,500 of Cognizant's 9,000 employees are in India. The rest are in smaller operations based in Ireland and Phoenix.

---

[46] *William Sherman, "City Tech Jobs Down Drain,"* New York Daily News *(June 1, 2003)*

[47] *"Lehman Moves Jobs from India,"* BBC News *(December 16, 2003)*

[48] *"Lehman Not to Curb Outsourcing,"* Business Standard *(January 1, 2004)*

[49] *Paul Mcdougall, "MetLife Weighs Offshore Option,"* InformationWeek *(December 17, 2003)*

[50] *Juan Carlos Perez, "Cognizant to Expand India Facilities, Grow Global Staff,"* Computerworld *(December 22, 2003)*

Allstate

Allstate has 39,284 employees worldwide. At the end of the third quarter of 2003, Allstate generated total revenue of close to $23.9 billion.

Allstate has 650 offshore employees in Northern Ireland who perform software maintenance and development.[51] Allstate originally launched its operations in Northern Ireland (via its subsidiary Northbrook Technology) to help deal with Y2K. The American contractors that the company had hired in Chicago were expensive, not to mention that half of them tended to leave for higher-paying work. By sending work overseas, Allstate is able to retain much of the domain knowledge and talent that it lost when contractors left.

Telecom

Have you ever driven by a telecom facility? They don't have any windows. That's because the buildings house nothing but hardware, hardware that runs in-house software and can be managed remotely.

Does this sound like a candidate for offshoring?

SBC

SBC employs 175,400 people worldwide. In 2002, SBC generated total revenue in excess of $43 billion.

SBC has tried very hard to keep its offshoring operations under wraps. For example, an offshore service provider named Cymbal, a Fremont company with offices in Bangalore and Hyderabad, was asked by SBC to sign a nondisclosure agreement. According to Helena Pechaver Starc, Cymbal's vice president of marketing, "There are very specific guidelines that no information should be in the press."[52]

This didn't stop an article about SBC's deal with Infosys, written by a man named Abhrajit Gangopadhyay, from appearing in the *Hindu Business Line* on May 30, 2003. The article's title, "Infosys Wins $60-M Order from U.S. Telecom Co" pretty much says it all. The six-year deal with SBC could land Infosys up to $10 million annually.

> **NOTE** This reminds me of how the media in the U.K. will often touch on topics that the media has blacked out in the U.S. Advertisers have power, but they can't always reach into other countries. If all else fails, look at sources overseas like the *BBC News* (`http://news.bbc.co.uk/`).

---

[51] *Julia King, "The Best of Both Shores,"* Computerworld *(April 21, 2003,* `http://www.computerworld.com/managementtopics/outsourcing/story/0,10801,80440,00.html`*)*

[52] *David Lazarus, "SBC Quietly Spins Off Jobs to India,"* San Francisco Chronicle *(October 31, 2003)*

While SBC has been making moves offshore, the company has begun to skimp on its American employees here in the U.S. San Francisco journalist David Lazarus discovered that in December 2003, SBC employees received a memo stating that trash pickups from cubicles would *be limited to at most once a week*. Lazarus commented, "This is a company, mind you, that reported profit of $5.6 billion last year and handed its chief exec, Ed Whitacre, $8.6 million in salary and bonuses. And that was with office wastebaskets still being emptied once a day."[53] The memo also stated that the cutbacks would hit air conditioning in the summer, heating in the winter, and the number of security guards on duty.

Cisco

Cisco employs over 34,000 people worldwide. For the financial year ending on July 26, 2003, Cisco had net sales of $18.8 billion.

Cisco employs 2,500 people in India who perform basic R&D and product development.[54] 500 of those people are full-time Cisco employees, and the rest are outsourced through third-party providers. According to Samu Devarajan, head of the company's India Global Development Center, "There is no other center in Cisco outside India where this large-scale engineering partnership is happening."[55]

Cisco has also made moves to offshore jobs to China. In October 2003, Cisco announced that it had entered into a technology support (read call center) outsourcing deal with a company in Beijing named Information Technology United Corporation (ITUC).[56]

AT&T

AT&T employed approximately 71,000 people worldwide in 2003. For the nine-month period ending on September 30, 2003, AT&T generated total revenue of $26 billion.

In December 2003, AT&T announced that it would be reducing its workforce by 12 percent (about 8,500 employees).[57] Chief Information Officer Christopher Corrado acknowledged that AT&T was using outside vendors to cuts costs and boost profit margins.[58] AT&T declined to comment on dealings with Wipro, Tata Consultancy Services, and other third-party providers.

---

[53] *David Lazarus, "SBC Talking Trash,"* San Francisco Chronicle *(December 24, 2003)*

[54] *Steve Tanner, "Heavyweights Sending R&D Overseas,"* Biz Ink *(August 29, 2003)*

[55] *John Ribeiro, "Analysis: In Shift, IT Vendors Outsource R&D to India,"* InfoWorld *(October 21, 2002,* `http://archive.infoworld.com/articles/hn/xml/02/10/21/021021hnindia.xml?s=IDGNS`*)*

[56] *Phelim Kyne, "INTERVIEW: Cisco China Deal Threatens India Outsourcing,"* Dow Jones Newswires *(October 20, 2003)*

[57] *"AT&T Ups Layoffs to 12 Percent from 10 Percent,"* Associated Press *(December 11, 2003)*

[58] *Brier Dudley, "More Layoffs Possible for AT&T Wireless; Some Jobs Go to India,"* Seattle Times *(November 20, 2003)*

Who's Helping Companies Go Offshore

With the potential to decrease cost structure and increase revenue, large American corporations have begun to take the plunge. Corporations overseas and here in the U.S., in addition to our own legislature, have all played a role in helping them do so. The new buzzword of the day is BPO, or Business Process Outsourcing. Another new acronym that's being used is ITES, for IT-Enabled Services. Sometimes when people talk about offshoring, they use the term *ITES/BPO*, or ITES-BPO.

Companies Based Offshore

India's three largest BPO service providers are Tata Consultancy Services (TCS), Wipro Ltd., and Infosys Technologies Ltd. TCS employs more than 24,000 people worldwide and has over 800 clients. Wipro employs 24,500 workers, serves over 300 corporate customers, and guarantees costs savings up to 35 percent for businesses that outsource with them. Infosys employs over 19,000 people worldwide and serves 345 clients. Table 2-5 offers a rundown of the relative size of these three offshore service providers.

Table 2-5 BPO Service Providers in India

BPO Service Provider	Head Count	Customers
TCS	24,000	800+
Wipro	24,500	300+
Infosys	19,000	345+

Although American clients may prefer not to publicize their deals, an interesting way to see who is offshoring is to examine the client lists that TCS, Wipro, and Infosys provide at their web sites. You should notice a lot of big names, some of which will be familiar. Once you've scanned through the lists, you'll understand how truly pervasive offshoring has become and the potential it has to affect our economy.

TCS Sample Client List

American Express	NACCO
American International Group	Nan Shan Life Insurance
Amoco Petroleum	NASD
Anglian Water	National Securities Depository
Asian Development Bank	National Stock Clearing Corporation
AT&T	Nedcor
AXA Insurance	Nike
Bahrain Airport Services	Nokia
Best Buy	Nortel Networks
Boeing	Northwest Airlines
Bombay Stock Exchange	Ohio Casualty Group
British Airways	P&O Nedlloyd
British Gas	PayServ
British Telecom	Pershing Technology Group
Canadian Depository for Securities	Prudential Insurance (U.S.)
Citibank	Punjab National Bank
Compaq	Qwest/US West
Credit Suisse First Boston	Racal
Credit Suisse Private Banking	Reserve Bank of India
Cummins	Retek
Dell Computer	Rockwell
Deutsche Bank	Royal Bank of Scotland
Dresdner Kleinwort Benson	SAAB
East Midland Electricity	Sainsbury's
Eaton	SBC Communications
EMC	Schlumberger
Far EasTone	Share Transaction Totally Electronic
Fidelity Investment	Singapore Airlines
Ford Motor	SIS SegaInterSettle
General Motors	Somerfield
Level3	Southern Company Services
Government of Sri Lanka	St. Paul Insurance

Continued

TCS Sample Client List

- Government Organization for Social Insurance, Saudi Arabia
- Hewlett-Packard
- Hindustan Aeronautics
- HSBC
- Husky
- IBM
- Indian Hotels
- Industrial Development Bank of India
- ING America
- JC Penney
- JD Williams
- Johnson & Johnson
- Kellogg's
- KLM
- Lifescan
- London Electric
- Lucent Technologies
- MAN B&W
- McGraw-Hill
- Michelin
- Microsoft
- Mpct Solutions
- Standard Chartered Bank
- Standard Life Assurance
- State of Montana
- State of Pennsylvania
- Swisscom
- Target Corporation
- Tata Steel
- Tata Teleservices
- Texas Instruments
- Thermo King
- Time Customer Service
- Tower Group Companies
- UBS
- Unigraphics Solutions
- Unit Trust of India
- Unocal
- U.S. Government—Department of Defense
- USAA
- Verizon Communications
- W.S. Atkins International
- Westpac Financial Services

Wipro Sample Client List

- ABN AMRO
- Alcatel
- Allianz Church & General
- Analog Devices
- Cisco
- Daiwa
- Morgan Stanley
- NCR
- NEC
- Nokia
- Nortel
- Skandia

Continued

Wipro Sample Client List

Embedded Systems
Epson
Ericsson
Farmers Insurance
Franklin Templeton
Fujitsu
HP
J.P. Morgan
Lucent
Magneti Marelli
Microsoft
Sony
StorageTek
Sun
Sun Microsystems
Texas Instruments
Thomas Cook
Thomson
Toshiba
Upaid
Winterthur

Infosys Sample Client List

Aetna
Airbus
Aon
Arcot Systems
Avici Systems
Avid Technology
AXA Online Japan
Blue Martini
Capro
Centrata
Cisco
Citadon
Citadon
CopperCom
Evolving Systems
Fairfax Financial Services
Huawei Technologies
i2 Technologies
JDS Uniphase
Microsoft
New York Life Insurance
NightFire Software
Nortel Networks
Northwestern Mutual Life Insurance
OnMobile Systems
Paradyne
QRS
Quintessent Communications
Riverstone Networks
SCT
Siemens Energy and Automation
SunAmerica
Suncorp Metway
Swiss Re
Syndesis
The Boeing Company
The LexisNexis Group
TIBCO

Continued

Infosys Sample Client List	
Jetstream Communications	Valeo
Johnson Controls	Valicert
Last Mile Solutions	Van Dorn Demag
Lucent Technologies	Vicorp
Marsh Canada	Yantra

NAASCOM

The National Association of Software Service Companies is a group of some 800 companies (including TCS, Wipro, and Infosys) in India that aims to promote the growth of offshore outsourcing.

According the NASSCOM FAQ on ITES-BPO, which you can view at the NASSCOM web site (`http://www.nasscom.org`), in 2003 approximately 171,000 people in India were employed as ITES-BPO professionals. This work generated approximately $2.35 billion of revenue, and represented an annual growth of 59 percent.

I like to think of NASSCOM as a cheerleader for Indian corporate interests. Naturally, everything that you see at its web site is geared towards encouraging offshore outsourcing in India.

American Service Providers

The largest U.S. BPO service providers include IBM (NYSE: IBM), Electronic Data Systems (NYSE: EDS), Accenture (the company formerly known as Andersen Consulting, NYSE: ACN), Unisys (NYSE: UIS), and Cap Gemini Ernst & Young. In this section, I'm going to throw a lot of numbers at you, primarily in an attempt to demonstrate how popular BPO has become. Naturally, offshore outsourcing is a part of this picture.

IBM facilitates outsourcing through its Global Services division. One of the products that IBM Global Services (IGS) provides is *Strategic Outsourcing*, which includes third-party management of business applications, web portals, data centers, network backbones, and desktop systems. This has proven to be a moneymaker for Big Blue. In late August 2003, IBM agreed to outsource Proctor & Gamble's employee services in a multiyear deal worth roughly $500 million.[59]

EDS offers BPO services for human resources, finance, accounting, content management, and procurement. EDS employs 138,000 people worldwide in 60 countries. EDS has over 35,000 clients, and in 2002 the company

[59] *Erin Joyce, "IBM Seen Snatching BPO Pact with P&G,"* Internetnews.com *(August 28, 2003,* `http://www.internetnews.com/ent-news/article.php/3070201`*)*

generated $21.5 billion in total revenue. EDS currently makes approximately $3 billion annually from BPO.[60]

Accenture employs about 86,000 people in 48 countries and earned net revenues of $11.8 billion for the fiscal year ended August 31, 2003. In 2003, the revenue that Accenture made from BPO doubled to $1.44 billion.[61] BPO customers of note for Accenture include AT&T and the U.S. Dept. of Defense. According to Accenture's fact sheet,[62] clients include "87 of the Fortune Global 100 and more than two-thirds of the Fortune Global 500."

In 2003, Unisys had 10,000 employees devoted to outsourcing worldwide. Since 2000, 7,000 employees were hired on as a result of outsourcing contracts. Unisys offers BPO services for payment processing (i.e., checks), insurance administration, claim processing, finance, and accounting. Unisys also offers IT infrastructure outsourcing and application management services.

Cap Gemini Ernst & Young employs 12,000 people worldwide with respect to its outsourcing operations. Like Unisys, the company's outsourcing operations are broken up into BPO, IT infrastructure outsourcing, and application management.

Our Legislators

Our legislators have conveniently ignored abuse of the visa program. At the end of 2003, the Department of Homeland Security couldn't tell me how many H-1B and L-1 visa holders are currently in the U.S.!

Part of the problem has to do with enforcement. The L-1 visa program wasn't intended to enable covert immigration; it was instituted to allow intra-company transfers of employees who had specialized knowledge (e.g., not generic programmers). Our government isn't aggressively pursuing abusers. As I mentioned in Chapter 1, Representative John Mica (R-Florida) received almost $4,000 in campaign contributions from Siemens between the time when Mike Emmons brought the company's abuse to his attention and the following elections.

On October 3, 2000, the House of Representatives and Senate voted to temporarily double the H-1B ceiling. After the vote was made, Senator Robert Bennett (R-Utah) stated, "There were, in fact, a whole lot of folks against it, but because they are tapping the high-tech community for campaign contributions, they don't want to admit that in public."[63]

Could it be any clearer? *The people who really run this country are the same people who control the capital.* Until this changes, large transnational corporations will continue to find ways to stymie our legal system. Professors

---

[60] *Juan Carlos Perez, "Update: EDS to Boost BPO Offerings,"* IDG News Service *(November 18, 2003)*

[61] *Thomas Hoffman, "Business Process Outsourcing Bolsters Accenture,"* Computerworld *(November 12, 2003)*

[62] `http://www.accenture.com/xd/xd.asp?it=enweb&xd=newsroom\fact_sheet.xml`

[63] *Carolyn Lochhead, "Bill to Boost Tech Visas Sails Through Congress,"* San Francisco Chronicle *(October 4, 2000)*

like Norman Matloff[64] and Ron Hira[65] have suggested extensive reforms, but their voices will be ignored until corporate interests are no longer able to effectively purchase legislation.

It's not just enforcement, however, it's also new legislation that's encouraging globalization of the labor force. For example, on May 6, 2003, the U.S. entered into a bilateral Free Trade Agreement (FTA) with Singapore (Public Law 108-78, 117 *Stat.* 948).

Hey, I wonder if the billion dollars that HP plans to invest in Singapore has anything to do with this?

Likewise, on June 6, 2003 the U.S. entered into the United States–Chile FTA (Public Law 108-77, 117 *Stat.* 909). These laws reserve a total of 6,000 visas (5,400 for Singapore and 1.400 for Chile), which is approximately 10 percent of the current H-1B limit (65,000).

To top it all off, President Bush wants to offer millions of illegal immigrants three-year guest worker visas if they can prove that they have a job in the U.S.[66] The White House's fact sheet on the program[67] stipulates that this would be limited to cases "when no Americans can be found to fill the jobs." Personally, this reminds me of the H-1B law that requires employers to pay H-1B visa holders the "prevailing wage."

President Bush's recommendations are so off the wall that even his fellow conservatives are speaking out against him. David Keene, chairman of the American Conservative Union, is quoted as saying, "The Bush administration would have us believe that this move toward legalizing the status of illegal immigrants—lawbreakers—will curb the flow of illegal immigration and enhance our border security. Nothing could be further from the truth."[68]

Looking Ahead: Various Studies, and a Word of Warning

After reading the previous sections, there should be no doubt that corporations are offshoring. The truly salient question is, just how prevalent is it going to become? There are a handful of studies that have been performed by the likes of Forrester Research and Gartner. In this section, I'm going to look at all of them. In terms of who's right and who's wrong, I'll let you decide for yourself, although I do think I should voice a few words of warning.

---

[64] *Norman Matloff,* Needed Reform for the H-1B and L-1 Work Visas: Major Points *(University of California Davis,* `http://heather.cs.ucdavis.edu/Summary.html`*)*

[65] *Testimony of Ron Hira to The Committee on Small Business, United States House of Representatives (*`http://www.ieeeusa.org/forum/POLICY/2003/102003.html`*)*

[66] *Steve Holland, "Bush Proposing Immigration Reform for Millions,"* Reuters *(January 6, 2003)*

[67] `http://www.whitehouse.gov/news/releases/2004/01/20040107-1.html`

[68] *"Immigration Quotes,"* Associated Press *(January 7, 2004)*

If there's one thing that bothered me, it's that no one seemed to provide a methodology for the projections they made. It's as if they pulled their results out of a hat or something. Presto . . . here's the future.

In academic research journals, you're required to provide the reader with your methodology and data set so that other researchers can reproduce your results, or perhaps bring them into question. I can tell you that from my background in physics, experimental replication is everything when it comes to credibility. If you can't reproduce a finding, the theory behind it is useless.

I suspect that most of these studies have precluded methodology information for this very reason; it allows their conclusions to be questioned. Oh no, they can't have that, they're experts.

In the introduction of this book, I mentioned the importance of being able to connect the dots on your own. Thus, you should take the following studies with a grain of salt for the very reason that they don't provide you with any dots. They simply provide you with a picture and force you to assume that they connected the dots correctly.

Caveat emptor.

Having formally issued this stern warning, ahem, let's look and see what the "experts" have to say about the future implications of offshoring.

Forrester Research

Title: "3.3 Million U.S. Services Jobs to Go Offshore"

Date: November 11, 2002

Author: John C. McCarthy, et al.

Of all the studies, this is the one most often quoted by the media. Not only that, but the study's lead researcher (John McCarthy) was cordial enough to e-mail me a copy. According to McCarthy, by the year 2015, it was projected that over 3.3 million white-collar jobs would be sent offshore. A breakdown of the figure is provided in Table 2-6.

Table 2-6 Outsourcing Through 2015

Job Category	2000	2005	2010	2015
Management	0	37,477	117,835	288,281
Business	10,787	61,252	161,722	348,028
Computer	27,171	108,991	276,954	472,632
Architecture	3,498	32,302	83,237	184,347
Life sciences	0	3,677	14,478	36,770
Legal	1,793	14,220	34,673	74,642

Continued

Table 2-6 *Continued*

Job Category	2000	2005	2010	2015
Art, design	818	5,576	13,846	29,639
Sales	4,619	29,064	97,321	226,564
Office	53,987	295,034	791,034	1,659,310
Total	**102,674**	**587,592**	**1,591,101**	**3,320,213**

Source: U.S. Department of Labor and Forrester Research, Inc.

As you can see, software isn't the only industry that will be affected. Office jobs, management, and general business positions are threatened. There are those who might say, "Look, 3.3 million people isn't that much. The government says that in the third quarter of 2003 there were approximately 147 million people employed in the private sector. This is a little over 2 percent of the current employment statistic. No big whoop."

Personally, I don't think 3.3 million is exactly a small number. According to the Census Bureau, Chicago has a population of approximately 3 million. Imagine the entire city of Chicago vanishing by 2015.

Not only that, but McCarthy has claimed that his estimates err on the side of caution. "What we did was size a trend that was out there," states McCarthy. "We tried to be conservative."[69] Cynthia Kroll, a researcher at Berkeley, concluded that "this translates to a little over 250,000 [jobs] per year, a number which seems conservative, based on the rate of outsourcing over the last few years."

As you'll see, after reading through the following studies, he *was* actually being cautious.

McKinsey Global Institute (MGI)

Title: "Offshoring: Is it a Win-Win Game?"

Date: August 2003

Not wanting to be left out of the fun, those shrewd MBA types at McKinsey have also put forward their own study. MGI doesn't offer an offshore headcount statistic so much as it downplays the potential for leaving Americans out in the cold. With regard to Forrester's prediction, McKinsey believes that an annual loss of over 250,000 jobs a year is an acceptable amount given the associated benefits.

MGI claims that savings from going offshore will allow displaced American workers to take new jobs. Specifically, MGI estimates that, once communication and management costs are taken into account, offshoring can provide

---

[69] *Steve Lohr, "Offshore Jobs in Technology: Opportunity or a Threat?"* New York Times *(Dec. 22, 2003)*

costs savings of at least 45 to 55 percent. Thus, for every dollar spent offshore, 45 to 55 cents are recovered as cost savings. This money then gets funneled back to investors, or is used to fund innovation via research and development.

MGI also claims that the shrinking demographic of working age Americans (age range 24 to 54) will result in a labor shortage and that offshoring can be used to resolve the shortage. This argument sounded suspicious to me, especially after reading Peter Cappelli's article, "Will There *Really* Be a Labor Shortage?" in *Organizational Dynamics*. Hence, I address this issue at length in Chapter 5 (at which point, you'll see the supposed "research" from MGI in a new light).

Gartner Research

Title: "U.S. Offshore Outsourcing: Structural Changes, Big Impact"

Date: July 15, 2003

Author: Diane Morello

This reports, among other things, predicts that by the end of 2004, half a million IT jobs will leave the U.S. for other countries. The report also predicts, with an 80 percent probability, that less than 40 percent of the people who lose their jobs will be redeployed by their employer.

Gartner cautions that business leaders shouldn't underestimate the impact of offshoring jobs. Over the long run, sending jobs overseas has the ability to stunt the supply of future talent and undermine the integrity of existing intellectual assets at home. Morello warns, "Identifying, capturing, and measuring core enterprise knowledge is daunting, especially when critical knowledge is often subordinate to technical skill sets."

Goldman Sachs & Co.

Title: "Offshoring: Where have all the Jobs Gone?" (*U.S. Economics Analyst*, no. 03/38)

Date: September 19, 2003

Author: Andrew Tilton

Over the next ten years, Tilton forecasts that up to 6 million service jobs could leave the U.S. This is twice the number that Forrester predicts.

Although Tilton admits that U.S. corporations will realize higher income and cost savings over the short term, it will not last forever. Tilton states that the migration of jobs overseas will increase U.S. imports and decrease the demand for U.S. labor, forcing the value of the dollar downwards. U.S. corporations may be able to boost short-term income levels via cost savings, but as time progresses competition will dissolve these gains.

Deloitte Research

Title: "The Cusp of a Revolution: How Offshoring Will Transform the Financial Services Industry"

Date: 2003

Author: Chris Gentile

Chris Gentile predicts that by 2008, roughly 2 million financial service jobs that currently exist in the U.S. are destined for offshore deployment. He calculates that this will generate an average cost savings of $138 billion.

According to Gentile, offshoring is a necessity because the financial institutes that don't use offshore labor will *appear* to be at a competitive disadvantage. The markets will respond to this impression of weakness and send their share price downward.

This train of thought reminds me of a quote from the Prince:

> *Men judge generally more by the eye than by the hand, because it belongs to everybody to see you, to few to come in touch with you. Every one sees what you appear to be, few really know what you are, and those few dare not oppose themselves to the opinion of the many.*

I suppose now we know why the markets are inefficient.

NASSCOM

Title: "The Impact of Global Sourcing on the U.S. Economy, 2003–2010"

Date: October 9, 2003

According to NASSCOM, the U.S. will face a labor shortage of 5.6 million workers by 2010. The report also predicts that this labor shortfall will cost the U.S. $2 trillion in growth opportunities and that 1.3 million jobs will move offshore from 2003 to 2010. This job loss estimate is a third of Forrester's.

Naturally, you should note that this is an organization that represents Indian business interests. Who do you suppose NASSCOM will recommend with regard to making up for this shortage of labor? Indian engineers?

Fisher Center for Real Estate and Urban Economics

Title: "The New Wave of Outsourcing" (University of California Berkeley)

Date: Fall 2003

Authors: Cynthia Kroll and Ashok Deo Bardham

Given that this is an academic paper, it should come as no surprise that methodology and experimental data are provided. I would expect no less from an institution like U.C. Berkeley. As such, this study is unique among those in this chapter.

Rather than predict how many jobs will leave the U.S., Kroll looks at how many jobs are *at risk* to leave the U.S. This creates an upper bound that can be used determine the maximum potential impact of offshoring. Rather than asking, "How bad will it be?" Kroll asks, "How bad can it be?"

Kroll started with 2001 employment data from the Bureau of Labor Statistics. Then she isolated job categories that she believed to be vulnerable to offshoring and simply totaled them up. What she found was that 11 percent of the U.S. working population were at risk for having their jobs sent offshore (see Table 2-7).

Table 2-7 Jobs at Risk of Being Sent Offshore

	Employment	Average Annual Salary
Total Employment	127,980,410	$34,020
Occupations		
Office support	8,637,900	$29,791
Computer operators	177,990	$30,780
Data entry keyers	405,000	$22,740
Business and financial support	2,153,480	$52,559
Computer and math professionals	2,825,870	$60,350
Paralegals and legal assistants	183,550	$39,220
Diagnostic support services	168,240	$38,860
Medical transcriptionists	94,090	$27,020
Total in outsourcing risk occupations	**14,063,130**	**$39,631**
Percent of all occupations		**11.0%**

Source: Fisher Center for Real Estate and Urban Economics

Bureau of Labor Statistics

Let's see what the BLS has to say with regard to the future. For the sake of keeping this under a page or so, I'm going to limit my discussion to the computer and mathematical science occupations. In other words, I'm going to restrict myself to a specific subset of Standard Occupational Classification (SOC) codes (150-1011 to 150-2091).

For the data shown in Table 2-8, I referenced an article by Daniel Hecker, entitled "Occupational Employment Projections to 2012," in the *Monthly Labor Review* (February 2004).

Table 2-8 Demand Forecast for Technical Positions

Title	2002	2012 (in Thousands)
Computer and information scientists, research	23	30
Computer programmers	499	571
Computer software engineers, applications	394	573
Computer software engineers, systems software	281	409
Computer support specialists	507	660
Computer systems analysts	468	653
Database administrators	110	159
Network and computer systems administrators	251	345
Network systems and data communications analysts	186	292
Actuaries	15	18
Mathematicians	3	3
Operations research analysts	62	66
Statisticians	20	21

Source: Bureau of Labor Statistics

All told, there will be a 35 percent increase in the number of computer and quantitative jobs (i.e., 3,018,000 in 2002 to 4,069,000 in 2012). To be honest, this doesn't necessarily jibe with what I see around me everyday. What's wrong?

Even the BLS can get things wrong. For example, the BLS's 2000–2010 predictions were tainted by dot-com hype, such that they predicted a 60 percent increase in IT jobs over ten years, as opposed to a 30 percent increase. That's not exactly a minor differential! Who's to say that relative changes in the 2004–2014 projections won't be as dramatic? According to George McClure, chairman of career and work force policy at the Institute of Electrical & Electronics Engineers, "It [the BLS] was way off. . . . Their crystal ball isn't much better than the rest of ours."[70]

[70] *Brian Deagon, "Demand for Engineers Rising Fast in U.S,"* Investor's Business Daily *(January 20, 2004)*

CHAPTER 3

The Offshoring Obstacle Course

Chapter at a Glance

- Deciding What to Outsource
- Well-Defined Scope
- Start with Small Victories
- Choosing to Go Offshore
- Choosing a Location
- Labor Pool Requirements
  - Infrastructure Requirements
  - Political Stability
  - Financial Considerations
  - Geographic Considerations
- Alternative Offshore Destinations
  - Ireland
  - Israel
  - Mexico
  - Russia
  - Singapore
- Service Provider vs. Dedicated Facilities
- Service Provider Requirements
- Accountability and Service-Level Agreements
- Using a Multihomed Approach

- ▶ Quality Control
- ▶ Lost in Translation
- ▶ Intellectual Property
  - ▶ Trade Secrets
  - ▶ Piracy
- ▶ General Security Concerns
- ▶ National Security
- ▶ Closing Remarks

Corporations that decide to offshore have a number of obstacles they must circumnavigate. In this chapter, I'm not going to discuss whether offshore outsourcing is a good thing or a bad thing (I deal with that later, trust me). Rather, I'm going to assume that outsourcing is an a priori decision and then go from there. In this chapter, on behalf of my publisher, I assume the neutral frame of reference of a management consultant whose only interest is to advise his client of potential problems. *This isn't Reverend Blunden speaking* (with the exception of the sections "Intellectual Property" and "National Security"). If you want my opinion, read Chapter 5.

Having said that . . . the first few things that an American corporation has to decide are which business processes it should outsource, the extent to which it should outsource, and whether or not it should go offshore at all or stay in the U.S. with a local outsource provider.

If a corporation has decided to go offshore, a destination must be chosen. India and China seem to be popular locations. As time passes, due to a number of economic and political forces, other contenders will enter the global labor arena.

In terms of arranging operations in a specific country, a corporation going offshore has to decide whether to use an established offshore service provider or to set up a dedicated corporate presence that the company will manage itself.

Once an offshore facility has been established and contracts have been finalized, the corporation in question must defend its good name by keeping a keen eye on its investment. In this regard, quality control, intellectual property rights, and general security issues are important.

Deciding What to Outsource

In theory, a corporation can outsource any activity for which it doesn't possess a distinct competitive advantage—the idea being that a corporation can rely on external service providers to perform all other business processes at less cost with comparable, or even superior, quality. Thus, hypothetically, a company could stick to doing one or two things (i.e., where it has strategic assets) and hand over everything else to outsource service providers. If BPO providers had their way, this is how all businesses would be run (much to their advantage).

In practice, I think that the nature of a business process determines if it will be a good candidate for outsourcing—which is to say that there are business processes that might not necessarily represent a strategic asset that still can't be outsourced. Specifically, business processes can be classified according to the amount of management effort they demand and the amount of intracompany coordination they entail (see Figure 3-1). Good candidates for being outsourced reside in the lower-left quadrant; they require very little management or interaction with other parts of the company. The lower-left quadrant represents low-risk business processes. Back-office work and customer contact falls into this part of the graph. It's true that call center people are communicating; it's just that they're communicating with customers and not their fellow employees.

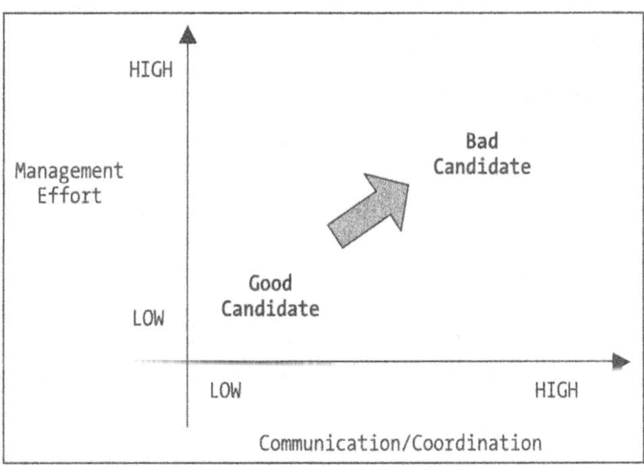

Figure 3-1 Candidates for outsourcing

Processes that necessitate significant management involvement, and a heavy volume of cross talk, aren't suitable candidates for being outsourced. These business processes reside in the upper-right quadrant of Figure 3-1. For example, a high-level sales team constantly has to be in touch with other parts of the company (e.g., product development, operations, accounting). They also need regular feedback and direction from upper management, sometimes on an hourly basis. This sort of tightly integrated business process needs to be right in the middle of things. Not to mention that sales people often have access to strategic information that shouldn't be disseminated to outsiders. High-level sales can't be outsourced effectively.

Processes that reside in the lower-right quadrant of Figure 3-1 require a significant amount of interaction but very little management effort. In this case, a company that relegates these processes to a BPO provider would be well advised to have a reliable, high-bandwidth networking system in place to facilitate things like teleconferencing, instant messaging, e-mail, and remote collaboration tools.

The upper-left quadrant (high management effort, low coordination) may seem like somewhat of an oddball. Companies that decide to outsource these activities would be well advised to involve a sizeable contingent of skilled managers who understand what needs to be done and are familiar with corporate best practices. Trying to manage remotely in this quadrant is risky: either commit an existing subset of managers or invest the resources necessary for training.

Well-Defined Scope

Once a company has decided to outsource a process, it must define the scope of the tasks involved. Not having a well-defined scope indicates that a company doesn't really have a clear understanding of its own business processes or how moving offshore will offer a tactical advantage. In this case, offshore outsourcing is probably more of a fashion statement, a product of the herd mentality, than a concrete financial decision. Corporations that take this approach won't realize cost savings and the associated benefits over the long run.

There's an old joke in the insurance industry: ask an actuarial consultant what time it is, and they'll tell you how to build a watch. Scope creep is a serious problem. It leads to budget overruns and delays. From a financial standpoint, it's in a consultant's best interest to increase their workload, and they will volunteer all sorts of ideas. For a company to protect itself from this sort of parasitic behavior, it has to have a very clear idea of what it wants done and what will be involved.

Start with Small Victories

Success breeds success. If a company hasn't previously climbed the BPO learning curve, it would be well advised to start by achieving a few small victories. This typically means undertaking missions that have the following attributes:

- Involves a short-term commitment
- Implements low-profile processes
- Involves work that is rules-based (not judgment-based) and noncore

- Includes static requirements
- Has access to an existing knowledge base

Short-term contracts are better because they limit the damage that can result from a bad deal. Not to mention that some industries change so rapidly (e.g., high-tech) that a long-term commitment is risky because the business conditions that an outsourcing agreement is based upon may no longer be valid.

Long-term agreements are also risky because service providers can become complacent if contract cancellation isn't a serious threat. For example, let's look at Blue Cross Blue Shield of Massachusetts (BCBSM). BCBSM has outsourced work to EDS for over 30 years. In the 1970s, BCBSM contracted EDS to manage its mainframe systems. As technology evolved, the company's arrangements with EDS expanded to cover the maintenance of its desktop systems. By the late 1990s, EDS had some 450 IT consultants working for BCBSM, which had only 150 in-house employees working on IT.[1]

BCBSM's habit of signing 10-year contracts with EDS had proved expensive. The company's per-member, per-month IT cost was $7.20, compared with an industry average (calculated by Gartner Group) of $3.50.[2] BCBSM's CIO at the time, Mark Caron, believed that EDS had "unfairly profited from the agreement for years, in contravention of a contract provision."[3]

Visibility is another factor. If an outsourcing project fails, it's better if it fails in the background where stockholders won't see it. This is the justification for skunk works projects. A *skunk works project* is an ambitious venture that is often not formally recognized or sanctioned. It lies outside the bounds of normal corporate activity. This gives the leaders who sponsor skunk works plausible deniability. Most skunk works projects don't exist, on paper, to begin. Only if a skunk works project succeeds is it brought out into the light for all to see.

> **NOTE** The term *skunk works* is derived from "Skonk Works," a small factory in the comic strip *Li'l Abner* that used skunks. The factory was horribly smelly, and consequently located out in the middle of nowhere. Lockheed's Advanced Development Projects Unit is unofficially referred to as "the skunk works."

The term *skunk works* doesn't imply failure; it implies secrecy and isolation. The creation of the Java programming language, for instance, was the side effect of a skunk works project at Sun Microsystems. CEO Scott McNealy directed James Gosling to go off and develop the next big thing. Gosling took his team, went to an undisclosed location across town, and set up a base of operation beneath the radar. No one but a small handful of people even knew

[1] *Lauren Gibbons Paul, "Insurer, Heal Thyself,"* CIO Magazine *(March 15, 2000)*

[2] *Ibid.*

[3] *Ibid.*

that Gosling and his team existed. If the project had been a complete failure, no one would have ever heard of it.

If a project is outsourced, it's less risky if the requirements remain static. Changing mission parameters typically demands both additional communication and management intervention, pushing the outsourced business process towards the upper-right quadrant of Figure 3-1. Change, in general, is dangerous. The annals of high-tech history are jam-packed with companies, like Osborne and Ashton-Tate, who went under because they failed to adapt to a changing environment. The high rate of change is also one reason why Warren Buffet claims value investing is problematic in the high-tech industry.

Finally, it's easier to outsource projects that are supported by an existing knowledge base. This could include design documentation, a paper trail recording the in-house employees initially involved, and white papers. Having access to these types of artifacts lowers the learning threshold and allows the outsource team to become productive more quickly.

Choosing to Go Offshore

Relying on someone else for domain experience and operational capabilities is an accepted, if not profitable, business practice. For example, Apple's PowerPC G5 relies upon IBM's 64-bit POWER4 processor. Apple can't afford to invest the resources to design and fabricate a processor by itself, given that it took over 300 engineers at IBM to design the chip,[4] and fabrication facilities cost $2.5 billion apiece[5] (more than Apple makes in a year). Although Apple's relationship with IBM is formally a business partnership, Apple is essentially outsourcing hardware development to IBM.

Thus, when an American corporation chooses to outsource within the U.S., it's usually to leverage domain expertise and economies of scale that can't be achieved in-house. Costs of labor and materials within the U.S. are comparable from one company to the next, so an onshore outsourcing company has to bring something else to the table that adds value to its service.

The fundamental benefit of offshore outsourcing is cost savings. This is what global labor arbitrage is all about; invest at a low price in one market and then sell at a high price in another market. An offshore outsourcing operation doesn't have to offer superior domain expertise or provide better quality service. Assuming that all other parameters are held at existing levels, an offshore operation only has to be cheaper to be attractive. Regardless of all the other reasons that companies use to justify going offshore (so that they don't look like sellouts), the underlying reason, upon which everything is based, is reducing cost structure.

---

[4] http://www-1.ibm.com/servers/eserver/pseries/hardware/whitepapers/power4.html

[5] http://www.gorr.state.ny.us/gorr/10_10_00gov_ibm.htm

Thus, if a company is going to outsource offshore, it needs to make sure that it takes the time to understand its existing cost structure so that it's aware of where standardization could result in improvements and so that it can successfully evaluate the savings that offshore providers offer.

Choosing a Location

Once a company has decided to send tasks offshore and determined which tasks are good candidates, a host country must be chosen. With regard to choosing a host, several criteria can be used to pick an optimal destination:

- Labor pool requirements
- Infrastructure requirements
- Political stability
- Financial considerations
- Geographic considerations

Labor Pool Requirements

The fundamental requirement for offshore outsourcing is the availability of cheaper labor substitutes. With regard to white-collar business tasks, this means a college-educated workforce. Countries that have recently made investments in their own educational systems, in addition to leveraging the educational system here in the U.S., have given themselves an advantage. This is one reason why U.S. corporations tend to target India and China as offshore destinations. In the 1999–2000 academic year, the United States produced 41,368 Ph.D.s (28 percent of which were noncitizens).[6] In 2002 the *People's Daily* newspaper stated that 37,000 Ph.D. candidates signed up for entrance exams in China.[7] Note they didn't indicate how many graduated, or even how many were accepted. This makes me a little suspicious of this figure (remember, this is a Chinese newspaper we're talking about).

The reason why education is so important is that training is expensive. Even though proper training is crucial to preserving quality of service, it's in a company's best interest to utilize a population that will ramp up quickly to business requirements.

Having a population that speaks English is a major selling point for India, which was a British colony until 1947. India has 15 official languages: Assamese, Bengali, Gujarati, Hindi, Kannada, Kashmiri, Malayalam, Marathi,

---

[6] *U.S. Department of Education, National Center for Education Statistics,* Digest of Education Statistics *(2002):Table 298*

[7] *"China May Have More Ph.D.s Than the U.S. in 2010,"* People's Daily *(October 22, 2002)*

Oriya, Punjabi, Sanskrit, Sindhi, Tamil, Telugu, and Urdu. About 30 percent of the population speaks Hindi, the national language.[8] However, English is used most often with respect to business communication.

The Indian population is also very young. This is a plus for potential employers who don't want to bother with providing health care benefits. According to the CIA *World Fact Book*, more than a third of India's population is less than 15 years old. The median age in India is 24.[9] Given that India's population tops 1 billion, this means that over 300 million people are less than 15 (more than the entire population of the U.S.). Compare this to the U.S., where a little over 20 percent of the population is less then 15 years of age (i.e., 58 million people out of 290 million), and the median age of the population is 36.[10] India's got about six times as many young people as the U.S.

Infrastructure Requirements

To enable remote communication with offshore operations (teleconferencing, e-mail, instant messaging, etc.), it helps if the host country has suitable digital and voice networks. Otherwise, the company outsourcing offshore will be required to fork over the cash necessary to build a dedicated infrastructure. Satellite earth stations aren't cheap.

Residential telephone service is a dubious proposition in India. The telephone density is roughly two for every 100 people.[11] The current waiting list for telephone service is over 2 million. This explains why India has erected nine satellite earth stations near its business centers (e.g., Bangalore, Hyderabad). India has eight Intelsat earth stations and one Inmarsat earth station.[12] India is also connected to the Fiber-Optic Link Around the Globe (FLAG). FLAG is a global, underwater fiber-optic cable system that winds its way from England to Japan. In the 1990s, the cable system was laid in a joint venture that included both AT&T and KDD Submarine Cable Systems.

India has 43 Internet service providers (ISPs) that provide access to over 7 million Internet users. Compare this to the U.S., which has 7,000 ISPs and over 165 million Internet users.[13]

Communication isn't the only infrastructure requirement. Host countries also need to have adequate transportation facilities and reliable utilities. For example, it would be difficult to do business in a region where workers couldn't commute to work or where electrical power was frequently cut off.

To help mitigate risk, corporations that go offshore should have contingencies in place to handle emergencies, preferable redundant systems elsewhere

[8] *Central Intelligence Agency,* World Fact Book 2003 *(Brasseys, Inc., 2003)*

[9] *Ibid.*

[10] *Ibid.*

[11] *Ibid.*

[12] *Ibid.*

[13] *Ibid.*

that offer a "hot" backup in case offshore services go down. A company called ALD offers a secure collocation site in Kent, England, which is a remodeled bunker. The building has 3-meter-thick concrete walls and 2-ton steel blast doors. The entire structure is shielded from electromagnetic threats (e.g., emanation detection, HERF) and onsite fuel storage allows the bunker to survive without external power for three months.[14]

Political Stability

On November 30, 1989, a bomb killed the chief executive of Deutsche Bank, Alfred Herrhausen, as he drove to work in his chauffeured Mercedes-Benz. Never mind that his vehicle was armored, and that two other support vehicles escorted him. Even the President of the United States, protected by the full force of the Secret Service, is vulnerable. If they really want to get you, they can.

Why make yourself an easy target?

The political stability of a destination can be a deal-breaker with regard to setting up an offshore presence. Who wants to establish a billion-dollar R&D facility in another country only to have it destroyed in a military conflict or "nationalized" by a radical political regime?

After India achieved independence from British rule, the continent was divided into a Muslim state (Pakistan) and a secular state (India). According to the *Indian Independence Act of 1947*, Kashmir was free to become a part of either Pakistan or India. After Kashmir acceded to India, fighting broke out and hostilities have existed since then. For instance, on December 13, 2001, five Islamic militants assaulted India's Parliament in New Delhi with explosives and gunfire. As both India and Pakistan massed troops on both sides of the border, the potential for escalation became real.

Both India and Pakistan have nuclear capabilities. In May 1998, India performed an underground nuclear weapons test, and Pakistan followed shortly afterwards. This wasn't India's first nuclear detonation either. India detonated its first nuclear device (the "Smiling Buddha") way back in 1974.[15]

While the possibility of a nuclear exchange doesn't seem to have scared away American businesses, other countries have had trouble attracting U.S. investors due to internal volatility.

For example, Southeast Asia has serious problems with terrorism. On October 12, 2002, bomb blasts ripped through the island of Bali in Indonesia killing over 180 people and injuring hundreds more. According to a travel warning issued by the U.S. State Department in August of 2003

---

[14] `http://www.thebunker.net`

[15] *"The Balance of Firepower,"* BBC News *(May 27, 1999)*

> *The U.S. Government believes extremist elements may be planning additional attacks targeting U.S. interests in Indonesia, particularly U.S. Government officials and facilities. As security is increased at official U.S. facilities, terrorists will seek softer targets.*

Imagine the kind of financial impact a terrorist organization could produce by bombing a semiconductor manufacturing facility?

NOTE Indonesia has the world's most dangerous waters. In 2003, there were 121 occurrences of piracy reported.[16] This isn't surprising, considering that a third of the world's trade sails through the Malacca Straits, which lie between Indonesia and Malaysia. In 2003, there were 28 occurrences of piracy on the Malacca Straits alone.[17]

The Philippines is a mixed bag when it comes to offshore outsourcing. On one hand, the Philippines produces 300,000 college graduates a year, all of which are fluent in English.[18] On the other hand, the Philippines suffer from serious problems with radical insurgents. With regard to the Philippines, the State Department cautions

> *The terrorist threat to Americans in the Philippines remains high, and the Embassy continues to receive reports of ongoing activities by known terrorist groups . . . Bombings have claimed many lives and injured hundreds in the Philippines during the past year, particularly on Mindanao. A bombing at a sports arena in Maguindanao Province on January 4, 2004, killed at least 15 persons and injured dozens more. A bombing at the international airport in Davao on March 4, 2003, killed at least 20 people, including one American, and injured over 140 others. Other explosive devices have been discovered and defused prior to detonation in these and other areas of Mindanao. The Government of the Philippines has condemned these incidents as acts of terrorism.*

With the inevitable proliferation of nuclear weapons, it's only a matter of time before a group of terrorists get their hands on a device and blow a city to kingdom come. Colonel Stanislav Lunev, the highest-ranking GRU agent ever to defect to the United States, came over to our side in 1992. He claims that during the Cold War, the GRU smuggled suitcase-sized nuclear weapons across the Mexican border into the U.S., with the intention of taking out our leadership in the event of hostilities.[19] A former official at the Pentagon has

---

[16] *Neil Chatterjee, "Piracy and Kidnapping Soar on the High Seas,"* Reuters *(January 28, 2003)*

[17] *Ibid.*

[18] *"Relocating the Back Office,"* The Economist *(December 11, 2003)*

[19] *Stanislav Lunev and Ira Winkler,* Through the Eyes of the Enemy: Russia's Highest Ranking Military Defector Reveals Why Russia Is More Dangerous Than Ever *(Regnery Publishing, 1998)*

advised me that if this is true, the tritium triggers have probably gone bad. Nevertheless, there is a risk that one of these suitcase-sized weapons might find its way into the wrong hands.

If the GRU was able to smuggle nuclear weapons across the U.S.–Mexican border during the height of the Cold War, imagine how easy it would be for a suicidal terrorist cell to smuggle a device across a border in India, or the Philippines, or . . .

Financial Considerations

Before a company moves offshore, it should deliberate over possible financial consequences. For example, if a company wants to pay its offshore employees in terms of the native currency, the fluctuation of foreign currency exchange rates must be taken into account. Depending on the circumstances, a company can make money or lose money; the key is to take this differential into account ahead of time.

Obviously, countries that don't require mandatory healthcare or retirement benefits, or have strict labor laws are more attractive from the perspective of cost structure. In the United States, employers must contribute, on average, about $6,656 a year to offer an employee insurance coverage for their family.[20] This is more than the total annual salary of some engineers in places like India and China.

Finally, some offshore destinations might be willing to offer American companies tax exemptions in an effort to attract their business. According to Kiran Karnik, president of NASSCOM, "I can't give numbers right now, but I know from personal conversations in the last three months that a number of MNCs have delayed their decision to set up BPO operations in India due to uncertainty on the tax front."[21] This goes to show that government intervention often has just as much to do with the economy as the supposed free market.

Geographic Considerations

Geographic distance is a factor that comes into play, regardless of what all of the ITES-BPO people say. For example, traveling from New York to Ireland is cheaper than traveling from New York to India, in terms of time and money. As an exercise, I looked up a few airfares online. Flying from New York City to Dublin costs around $418 with Air France and the estimated flight time was 11 hours. Flying from New York City to Bangalore with Air India cost $1,227 with a flight time of 17 hours. For executives who have to make frequent trips back and forth between the U.S. and the offshore destination, this can make a big difference.

---

[20] *Kaiser Family Foundation,* Employer Health Benefits 2003 Annual Survey

[21] *Aparna Kalra, "BPOs Should Get Tax Exemption,"* Times News Network *(January 14, 2004)*

Culturally, Ireland also tends to be less of a shock than India. There are pubs in Ireland, and there are pubs here in the U.S. The only difference is, the pubs in Ireland are better. Order up a Guinness, play a few rounds of darts, and you'll feel right at home.

The time zone differential is another thing to keep in mind, especially if you want to teleconference. At 9:00 a.m. in San Francisco, it's 5:00 p.m. in Dublin and it's past 10:00 p.m. in New Delhi. Unless your Indian programmers enjoy working evenings, scheduling a meeting will be difficult.

Alternative Offshore Destinations

India and China are the current undisputed champions of offshore outsourcing due to the low wage levels in each country and their enormous pools of labor. The runner-ups in the global labor market include nations like these:

- Israel
- Ireland
- Mexico
- Russia
- Singapore

The following discussion will examine what makes these nations second-tier offshore outsourcing providers. Table 3-1 should offer some initial clues.

Table 3-1 Comparing the U.S. to Offshore Destinations

Country	GDP Per Capita	Population	Telephone Main Lines	Internet Users
USA	$36,300	290 million	194 million	165 million (57%)
China	$4,700	1.3 billion	135 million	46 million (4%)
India	$2,600	1 billion	28 million	7 million (0.7%)
Israel	$19,500	6 million	2.8 million	2 million (30%)
Ireland	$29,300	3.9 million	1.6 million	1.3 million (33%)
Mexico	$8,900	105 million	12 million	3.5 million (3%)
Russia	$9,700	145 million	30 million	18 million (12%)
Singapore	$25,200	4.6 million	1.9 million	2.3 million (50%)

Source: *CIA* World Fact Book

Also, recall the average annual IT salary data from Chapter 1, as repeated here in Table 3-2.

Table 3-2 Average Annual IT Salary by Country

Country	Average Salary
USA	$61,630
Singapore	$33,504
Ireland	$23,000–$34,000
Israel	$15,000–$38,000
China	$8,952
India	$5,880–$11,000
Russia	$5,000–$7,500
Mexico	$1,400

Source: Stephanie Overby, "A Buyers Guide to Offshore Outsourcing," CIO Magazine *(November 15, 2002)*

Ireland

Ireland is very similar to the U.S. in terms of language and culture. Ireland is also relatively close to the U.S. (compared to India or Russia). The country has a solid communications infrastructure and a skilled labor pool. The local government has also taken steps to encourage Ireland's move towards a service-based economy. For instance, the Irish Council for Science, Technology, and Innovation (ICSTI) has set up a £250 million fund to encourage the development of high-tech skills in the third-level education sector.[22]

Because of all these factors, which make the transition easier for American corporations, U.S. companies will pay a premium for services in this country.

Israel

Israel could be considered the high-tech hub of the Middle East. This is due primarily to military conflicts that assailed Israel in its early days. The government realized that the country's security rested on its ability to independently develop military technology (several other Middle Eastern nations depend upon the U.S. for military hardware). By the early 1970s, Israel was manufacturing its own fighter jet, the Kfir. In 1988, Israel was the eighth country to independently send a satellite into orbit. According to the Ministry of Foreign Affairs, Israel spends 2.2 percent of its GDP on research and development

[22] `http://www.forfas.ie/icsti/statements/250inv/summary.htm`

(Israel is surpassed only by Japan and Sweden in this regard).[23] High-tech and technology-rich products account for 70 percent of Israel's exports.

In addition to a high degree of English proficiency, the CIA's *World Fact Book 2003* states, "Israel has a technologically advanced market economy with substantial government participation." This means that the Israeli government is more than willing to offer incentives to high-tech corporations that want to move offshore.

Intel Corporation has made significant investments in Israel.[24] Intel has design and development centers in Haifa, Yakum, and Petach Tikva. Intel also has fabrication facilities in Jerusalem (Fab 8) and Qiryat-Gat (Fab 18). These are nontrivial investments. Constructed in the late 1990s, the Qiryat-Gat Fab cost $1.6 billion to build. Of this amount, the Israeli government put up $600 million and Intel put up $1 billion. The Qiryat-Gat Fab employs over 2,000 people.

On the downside is the bitter Israeli-Palestinian conflict, which has been going on for decades and shows no immediate sign of letting up. Unfortunately, suicide bombings are a fact of day-to-day life in Israel.

Mexico

Like Ireland, Mexico is close (very close). It also has the benefit of offering very cheap labor. These are Mexico's primary strategic advantages: proximity and cost. The problem is that these are the only real concrete benefits. The language barrier in Mexico is an issue, especially when you consider the abundance of English speakers in India. The availability of high-end expertise is also limited.

Russia

In December 1991, the Soviet Union splintered into 15 separate republics. Russia's transformation from a Communist dictatorship to a free enterprise economy has been rocky. The once world superpower is now at the mercy of a handful of oligarchs (read robber barons). The shift to private ownership was more like a land grab, creating a select group of powerful business interests. I'm talking about men like oil tycoon Mikhail Khodorkovsky, Russia's wealthiest man (according to *Forbes*), who was jailed on October 25, 2003, for fraud and tax evasion charges.[25]

Foreign investment in Russia came to $2.6 billion in 2002. This is up from $2.5 billion in 2001[26]—not very much, considering that there are corporations in the U.S., like Intel, that generate more net income than this. The dearth of

---

[23] http://www.mfa.gov.il/mfa/home.asp

[24] http://www.intel.com/jobs/israel/sites/

[25] *Steve Gutterman, "Moscow Court Keeps Oil Magnate in Jail,"* Associated Press *(January 15, 2004)*

[26] *Sabrina Tavernise, "Glimmers of an Investor-Friendly Russia,"* New York Times *(February 15, 2003)*

foreign investment reflects the lack of trust that multinationals have in Russian institutions and the underlying economic base. According to the CIA's *World Fact Book 2003*, "Oil, natural gas, metals, and timber account for more than 80 percent of exports, leaving the country vulnerable to swings in world prices." Compare this to Israel's high-tech export figure.

In addition to suffering from political and economic instability, Russia has the added disadvantages of the language barrier. Russia's communication infrastructure is weak in remote parts of the nation, and doing something as simple as establishing a dial-up connection can be a risky proposition.

On the upside, the Cold War left Russia with a large supply of talent in the hard sciences. Recall that Russia was once considered a military superpower; they had thousands of long-range ICBMs deployed, just like we did. Many of the people who were a part of this infrastructure have gone into IT, and can offer the kind of high-end skills that places like Mexico lack.

Singapore

Singapore is smaller than Israel; the country resides on an island the size of Washington, D.C. However, it's also one of the busiest ports in the world. Singapore has an extensive communications infrastructure (half of the population is Internet literate). In addition, as a former British trading colony, English is an official language.

Singapore has a considerable high-tech industry. According to the Singapore Ministry of Trade and Industry, from 1990 to 1998 the value of domestic high-technology exports increased from $24 billion to $62 billion and direct foreign investment rose 19 percent.

Given the advanced skill level of the working population, and the relatively higher standard of living, corporations setting up outposts here will pay the kind of money that they would in Ireland. In fact, it's gotten to the point where corporations in Singapore are outsourcing work to India. At the time of this book's writing, the Singapore Ministry of Trade and Industry reports that the seventh round of negotiation has been completed on the India-Singapore Comprehensive Economic Co-Operation Agreement (CECA).

Service Provider vs. Dedicated Facilities

Once a company has selected an offshore destination, it has to decide whether it wants to utilize local outsource providers in the destination country, or invest in its own dedicated facilities. This is strictly a function of a company's know-how and the degree of control that it desires.

If a corporation has had operations in a particular country for a few years, it may have enough experience to save money by precluding a third party.

Also, there may be instances in which a company wants to have exclusive control over a business process due to the involvement of U.S.-specific regulations or laws. If tight service-level agreements aren't good enough, and a corporation wants to be able to monitor offshore labor in real time and onsite, it may be wiser to shell out the cash to set up a dedicated base of operations.

Service Provider Requirements

If an American corporation feels comfortable enough to surrender control of a business process to an offshore provider, it can use several criteria to evaluate potential candidates:

- Domain expertise
- Track record
- Flexibility

Offshoring call center and back-office work is one thing. This type of work is easy to standardize and doesn't involve an in-depth understanding of protocols. Offshoring shared-infrastructure and knowledge-based work is different; it typically requires familiarity with regulations and laws that are country, if not state, specific. This type of domain proficiency requires years to acquire.

John McCarthy, a group director at Forrester Research, warned at a NASSCOM event in the fall of 2003 that, in an effort to be taken seriously by clients, BPO vendors overstate and embellish their domain expertise. According to McCarthy, almost 40 percent of the Fortune 1000 companies surveyed were aware that this occurred.[27] Thus, a corporation sending work offshore should be sure to stipulate, via service-level agreements, that specialized work be done only by properly accredited professionals (e.g., CPA, CFA Level III, state bar member).

Evaluating the track record of an offshore service provider is tricky. Naturally, vendors will all claim that they have an excellent record. They'll sweep failures under the rug and inflate their successes. Asking offshore service providers to offer realistic appraisals of their product is like asking students to grade their own test; they'll give themselves an "A" every time.

Word of mouth is one approach. This means finding clients and asking them for an honest evaluation. The problem with this approach is that translates into a serious investment if you want to talk to a decent subset of clients (e.g., TCS has had hundreds of customers). Another approach is to rely on industry organizations like Gartner Group, who'll do the footwork and then pass on their findings to you for a price.

Finally, there's flexibility. The offshore service provider should be able to accommodate changes as they occur. Specifically, an offshore service provider

---

[27] *"BPO vendors overrate expertise,"* The Hindu Business Line *(October 10, 2003)*

should be able to flawlessly scale upwards. Here's an example: in 1989, the state of Florida hired EDS to design a system for the state's Department of Health and Rehabilitative Services (HRS). As the transaction load reached 4 million transactions a day, the system started to crash and exhibit reliability problems. In 1992, HRS sued EDS for $65 million damages, citing a breach of warranty.

A service provider should also have the ability to shift operations back to the client company if necessary. This could be part of an exit plan, if the outsourcing arrangement doesn't work out. Or it could allow a company to take back control of its operations once it feels it has climbed the learning curve.

Accountability and Service-Level Agreements

Offshore outsourcing doesn't mean giving total control to the service provider. An acceptable level of control can be maintained through service-level agreements. A *service-level agreement* (SLA) is a contract between the recipient and provider that dictates the terms of service. It specifies the needs of the recipient, and establishes a set of shared expectations. An SLA is intended to help minimize disputes and moderate them when they occur.

For example, an SLC spells out general things like

- What tasks will be performed
- What the timeframe is for completion of the tasks
- What metrics will be used to track performance
- What acceptable thresholds are for these metrics
- How these metrics will be tracked and reported
- How disputes will be resolved
- Under what circumstances service will be terminated
- How operations will be shifted back to the recipient

There are context-sensitive specifics that need to be spelled out. For example, the SLA for an offshore software project might also stipulate

- A list of deliverables
- A roadmap specifying release dates
- The hourly rate to be paid, with a ceiling on total billable hours
- Conditions for payment based on meeting project milestones

An SLA is the legal equivalent of the carrot and the stick. It enumerates a detailed set of incentives, rewards, and punishments to protect the recipient from mission failure and encourage the offshore service provider to produce an outcome that results in a win-win scenario.

However, an SLA shouldn't be so restrictive that it doesn't accommodate changes. As I mentioned in the previous section, business environments change. For example, if an offshore operation is in the process of growing its facilities to scale upwards, it might not be fair to require it to adhere to the old metrics that applied when it was smaller.

Using a Multihomed Approach

Scarcity is one half of the supply-demand relationship that modern economic theory is based upon. In Douglas Adam's book *The Restaurant at the End of the Universe*, the inhabitants of prehistoric earth use leaves as a form of currency. To preserve their value, they go on a massive campaign of deforestation.

If you are the sole supplier of a scarce commodity, one that people need to survive (like water), then they're dependent upon you. While this sort of dependency gives the supplier leverage, it also makes the consumers of the commodity extremely vulnerable.

Shortly after Robert McNamara was appointed Secretary of Defense, he recognized that one of the biggest drains on public funding in the defense industry was the fact that contracts often had only a single supplier. In the absence of alternatives, it was hard to determine whether prices were fair or not. McNamara instituted a policy known as *second-sourcing*, which dictates that every part should have at least two suppliers.

This policy isn't limited to the defense industry. When IBM was designing the original PC, the company required Intel to second-source the 8088 processor. Intel ended up giving second-source rights to its longtime rival AMD.

In light of all this, if a company is going to outsource offshore, it's well advised to use multiple service providers in multiple locations. The motives, in this case, are both performance and cost. Recently, salaries are on the rise in India. Average annual salary increases in the ITES industry were 12.1 percent in 2002 and 15.4 percent in 2003.[28] This is twice the increase experienced by the second-place runner-up, the Philippines.[29] If the trend continues, eventually the cost savings of doing business in the country will disappear and corporations will be forced to go elsewhere.

To an extent, this is already occurring. For example, New York City used to rely on India to process its parking tickets until it discovered a cheaper supplier. NYC parking tickets are now sent more than 5,000 miles to an office in a

---

[28] *"IT Pros' Pay Packet Got Heftier in '03: Nasscom,"* Economictimes.com *(December 15, 2003)*

[29] *"Indian Pay Rises Highest in Asia,"* BBC News *(November 12, 2003)*

city named Accra, the capital of Ghana.[30] Workers in Ghana are paid $70 per month, more than twice the average per capita income.[31] Implementing offshore operations in different countries helps to guard against rising wages.

Quality Control

In 1998, AT&T agreed to pay a fine of $300,000 dollars for slamming long distance customers.[32] Over a six-month period stretching from 1997 through 1998, the Public Utility Commission of Texas received more than 400 complaints from customers who had been slammed. It just so happens that AT&T was using outsourced contractors to market its long distance services.

Given that corporations prefer not to publicize their dirty laundry, you won't find much in the papers about offshore outsourcing failures. Occasionally, something slips through the cracks. For example, customer complaints prompted Dell to move call center jobs back to the U.S. from India in November 2003.[33] Specifically, support for Dell's OptiPlex desktop model and Latitude notebook computer was sent back home.

Quality control mechanisms are necessary to protect a company's brand and customer base. Some business types believe that if metrics don't exist for a specific business process, then it shouldn't be outsourced. This isn't a bad idea.

Quality control metrics should be specified explicitly in the SLA, along with how they will be tracked (e.g., in real-time, daily) and archived. Some business process outputs, like labor costs, are easy to measure. Other process outputs, like customer satisfaction, are more difficult to quantify. It's the responsibility of the client to define a set of metrics and then settle on a set of benchmarks that delineate acceptable ranges.

> **NOTE** It's vital that the client company *not* relegate measurement tracking and analysis duties to the offshore BPO service provider. This is like asking students to grade their own tests. QC tracking and analysis should be kept in-house and under control of the client.

Naturally, the best medicine is preventative medicine. Proper training is the cheapest way to maintain service levels. The problem with training is that it's expensive. Training employees properly requires an up-front investment, and less scrupulous BPO providers may be tempted to skimp on training in an

---

[30] *Robert F. Worth, "In New York Tickets, Ghana Sees Orderly City,"* New York Times *(July 22, 2002)*

[31] *Ibid.*

[32] *Public Utility Commission of Texas (PUCT), news release (September 24, 1998)*

[33] *Amy Schatz, "Dell Sending Some Jobs Back to U.S.,"* Austin American Statesman *(November 21, 2003)*

effort to scavenge short-term gains. The best way to ensure proper training is to embed it as a clause in the SLA.

With respect to IT QA, there are a number of frameworks that service providers can use to differentiate themselves—e.g., ISO 9000, Software Capability Maturity Model (SCMM), IT Infrastructure Library (ITIL). A glance at Table 3-3 should help explain why India and China are considered prime offshore destinations.

Table 3-3 ISO Certifications by Country

Country	ISO 9000
China	75,755
USA	38,927
India	8,110
Singapore	5,379
Ireland	2,845
Mexico	2,508
Russia	1,710

Source: ISO Survey 2002

Lost in Translation

Of all the service-based work that has been sent offshore to India, call centers are the most easily recognizable. Any American who has made a call to a help line knows what I'm talking about. Call centers are a central pillar of the Indian BPO economy. Since 2000, the number of call centers in India has risen from 50 to 800.[34]

As I mentioned earlier, some outputs of process execution are difficult to measure, like the response an American consumer will have when they end up speaking to someone with a foreign accent. Given that collecting metrics are problematic in this scenario, training is crucial.

According to a study initiated by Professor Rosemary Batt, a researcher at Cornell University, Indian call centers tend to hire employees with a higher level of education and then invest more in their training.[35] Indian hires, on the

---

[34] *"Call Centres 'Bad for India,'"* BBC News *(December 11, 2003)*

[35] *Global Call Center Research Project (*`http://www.ilr.cornell.edu/cahrs/FacultyResearch.html`*)*

average, participate in 5.5 weeks of initial training and 3.5 weeks of ongoing training per year.[36]

Trainers are paid well, relatively speaking. A call center agent makes about $175 dollars per month.[37] Trainers can earn $315 to $375 a month at the outset and $950 to $1,000 a month with a couple of years of experience under their belt.[38]

Trainees learn techniques aimed at "accent neutralization" by watching American movies, sports, sitcoms, and news programs. It reminds me of a David Cronenberg movie called *Videodrome*, where television is used as a device to assimilate indigent people back into society. In other words, television engenders a level of reality that is more accurate and has more substance than that of everyday life.

To help complete the illusion, Indian call centers allow their employees to pick Western pseudonyms.[39] Charulekha becomes "Cassidy," and Chudamani becomes "Clark." Keep this in mind the next time you call up a help line. That ambiguous sounding service agent named "Jim Westwood" may actually be a heavily coached foreign national named Bharat Ramadorai.

Intellectual Property

Don't let your employees do to you what you did to your former boss.

—Intel General Counsel Roger Borovoy

Intellectual property (IP) is a general term used to refer to ideas, creations, or processes whose ownership is conferred by various legal constructs (e.g., copyright, patent, or trademark). IP crimes come in three different flavors:

- Trade secret theft
- Piracy (copyright violation)
- Counterfeiting (trademark infringement)

In this section, I'm going to look at the two types of IP crimes that assail the high-tech industry in particular: theft of trade secrets and piracy.

---

[36] *NASSCOM Newsline (December 2003,* `http://www.nasscom.org/bponewsline/research.asp`*)*

[37] *"Call Centres 'Bad for India,'"* BBC News *(December 11, 2003)*

[38] *"Call-Center Workers Straddle Two Continents and Cultures," Knowledge@wharton.com (*`http://knowledge.wharton.upenn.edu/100902_ss4.html`*)*

[39] *Michael Goldstein, "Customer Call Center Jobs Exported from U.S. to India,"* New York Daily News *(January 20, 2003)*

Trade Secrets

On July 16, 1945, the U.S. detonated the first nuclear weapon at a test site in at Alamogordo, New Mexico. Roughly four years later, on August 29, 1949, the Soviets detonated their first nuclear bomb. Somebody in the U.S. program had loose lips, and it didn't take long to find out whom it was. In 1950, Klaus Fuchs admitted that he gave secrets to the Soviets and was imprisoned for nine years. In 1953, Julius and Ethel Rosenberg were executed for passing secrets concerning the American nuclear program to the Soviets.

Over a period of 20 years, starting sometime in 1979, FBI agent Robert Hanssen passed intelligence to the KGB. By all accounts, he has caused more damage than any other American spy in public history. According to David Vise, author of a book on Hanssen entitled *The Bureau and the Mole*, Hanssen gave up the "crown jewels" of U.S. intelligence, including the "Continuity of Government Plan," which would be implemented in the event of a nuclear exchange; the national intelligence budget (which specifies intelligence activities); and the names of over 50 Russian agents.

As I hope these examples demonstrate, having sensitive information compromised is a serious issue. However, theft of proprietary information isn't just a threat to our federal government, it's also a threat to multinational corporations.

But how much of a threat is it? According to the *Intelligence Authorization Act for Fiscal Year 1995* (Public Law 103-359), "Reports On Foreign Industrial Espionage" (section 809), the U.S. president has to submit a yearly report to Congress "to improve the awareness of United States industry of foreign industrial espionage and the ability of such industry to protect against such espionage."

The name of the report that he submits is called the *Annual Report to Congress on Foreign Economic Collection and Industrial Espionage*. The Office of the National Counterintelligence Executive (NCIX) publishes this report. I retrieved the 2002 edition, which covers 2001, of this report online.[40] The report claims, "Some 75 countries were involved in one or more suspicious incidents." In terms of financial loss, the report states that "Private estimates put the combined costs of foreign and domestic economic espionage, including the theft of intellectual property, as high as $300 billion per year and rising." That's roughly 15 percent of the 2003 federal budget of $2.1 trillion.[41]

The External Threat

There are a number of ways that outsiders can pilfer information from U.S. corporations. The most popular technique, and the simplest, is to simply ask for it directly. Unsolicited requests for information and unsolicited requests to

---

[40] http://www.ncix.gov/news/2003/may/Annual_Economic_Report_Version.pdf

[41] http://www.whitehouse.gov/omb/budget/fy2003

purchase technology accounted for half of all suspicious incidents in 2001.[42] Competitive analysis professionals in particular like this trick because it's legal. Approximately 70 percent of information requests were made via e-mail,[43] which allowed the requests to be made with a degree of anonymity.

Yet another tactic is to offer services to U.S. companies that have access to proprietary trade secrets. The most common variation of this approach involves a foreign scientist applying for work with a U.S. company that has access to sensitive technology. The NCIX reports that in 2001, "[In] 15 percent of all suspicious incidents reported by cleared government contractors, foreign collectors attempted to insinuate themselves or their products into positions where they might gain access to high-tech goods."[44]

In the case of offshoring, information collectors don't even have to leave their own country. They simply hire themselves out to an offshore service provider, and the information comes to them.

The Internal Threat

Take another look at the quote that I began the section with. Offshore outsourcing introduces the danger that foreign researchers who work in other countries for U.S. corporations (e.g., Microsoft, Intel, HP, GE, and Motorola are all doing R&D offshore) will quit and then take their mind share and expertise with them to local indigenous companies, resulting in a massive shift of technological know-how.

They don't necessarily have to steal anything. They can legally take an existing idea and re-create an improved version. All of the experience and expertise that they developed walks right out the door. For example, when Dave Cutler left Digital Equipment Corporation in 1988 to design Windows NT for Microsoft, he had already designed a number of operating systems, including VAX/VMS, RSX-11M, and VAXELN.[45] Bill Gates was able to leverage Cutler's skill to build the industry's most prolific commercial software platform.

It's naive to think that this won't happen; it's just a matter of time. Not even a mountain of nondisclosure agreements will stop this sort of leakage. Before you know it, nations like China and India will have the know-how to compete against us, in terms of innovation and creativity, and win.

Piracy

Microsoft has touted its "product activation" scheme as a way to discourage piracy. The next iteration of Windows, code name Longhorn, is also being

---

[42] *Office of the National Counterintelligence Executive,* Annual Report to Congress on Foreign Economic Collection and Industrial Espionage–2002

[43] *Ibid.*

[44] *Ibid.*

[45] `http://www.microsoft.com/PressPass/exec/de/default.asp#DaveCutler`

marketed as a secure computing environment (the official term is *trustworthy computing*). This didn't seem to stop Malaysian software pirates, who have been selling copies of Longhorn for $1.58.[46] Piracy is both a profitable crime because of the low overhead and the high profit margin. Anyone with a CD burner can copy software. The NASSCOM Piracy FAQ reports that 41 percent of businesses in India use pirated software in 2001–2002. Table 3-4 displays the percentage of pirated software installations for a number of countries in 2002.

Table 3-4 Pirated Software Installations

Country	Percentage of Pirated Installations
China	92
Malaysia	70
India	64
Singapore	51
USA	25

Source: NASSCOM Piracy FAQ

According to the International Intellectual Property Alliance (IIPA), a consortium of more than 1,300 U.S. Corporations, the U.S. lost $9.2 billion in 2002 due to copyright violations.[47] The IIPA points out the Ukraine, China, India, and Southeast Asia as notable violators. The Ukraine in particular has a piracy rate in excess of 90 percent coupled with a very weak level of law enforcement.

The problems presented by piracy are exacerbated by the lack of solid international intellectual property laws. In fact, the FBI states that "international enforcement of IP laws is virtually nonexistent."[48]

The World Trade Organization has introduced legislation in the form of the *Agreement on Trade-Related Aspects of Intellectual Property Rights* (TRIPS). However, TRIPS measures can only be enforced locally. This means that multinational corporations that want to prosecute offenders will have to find ways to encourage local law enforcement officials in a foreign country to cooperate. Thus far, WTO members like China and India are also some of the worst offenders.

---

[46] *"Asian Pirates Sell Microsoft's Next Windows System,"* Reuters *(December 1, 2003)*

[47] *International Intellectual Property Alliance*, 2003 Special 301 Report on Global Copyright Protection and Enforcement (`http://www.iipa.com/special301_TOCs/2003_SPEC301_TOC.html`)

[48] `http://www.fbi.gov/hq/cid/fc/fifu/about/about_ipc.htm`

General Security Concerns

In an outsourcing chain that snaked through three different subcontractors, a Pakistani woman performing medical transcription on behalf of UCSF Medical Center tried to extort money from a patient. The transcriber, Lubna Baloch, warned

> *Your patient records are out in the open to be exposed, so you better track that person and make him pay my dues or otherwise I will expose all the voice files and patient records of UCSF Parnassus and Mt. Zion campuses on the Internet.*[49]

This brings to light two important points: First, outsource service providers should know who they are ultimately giving work to, so that they can assign accountability if need be. Second, once information goes overseas, confidential data is at greater risk. As I stated earlier, the link between law enforcement agencies on an international level is weak at best. This makes it easier for an extortionist to evade capture. The police in the U.S. already have a hard enough time when a crime is spread out among different counties. Imagine how hard it's going to be to prosecute a person whose crime is spread out across international borders.

When work is sent offshore, there's also the risk that an engineer in another country would embed a snippet of malicious code in the software that they build. As things stand now, we can't seem to deal with unintentional security holes; the addition of intentional security problems would significantly compound this situation.

On July 22, 2003, the director of information assurance (think NSA), Dan Wolf, presented a statement to the House Select Committee on Homeland Security. Wolf stated that "It has been estimated that over 90 percent of all successful attacks on DoD systems are based on vulnerabilities that are already known and that have an updated software fix or 'patch' available. . . . There is little coordinated effort today to develop tools and techniques to examine effectively and efficiently either source or executable software."[50]

The lesson, in this case, is that companies using offshore programmers should invest the resources necessary to perform exhaustive security audits. This should be stipulated in the SLA to ensure that the audits are done.

---

[49] *David Lazarus, "A Tough Lesson on Medical Privacy: Pakistani Transcriber Threatens UCSF over Back Pay,"* San Francisco Chronicle *(October 22, 2003)*

[50] `http://www.nsa.gov/ia/index.cfm`

National Security

The longer term objective [of industrial espionage] appears to be to enable their military establishments to move closer to parity with the United States and to give their defense-industrial base and private companies a competitive edge in the global economy.

—Office of the National Counterintelligence Executive

When the problem becomes obvious, it will be too late—and the outcome will be too depressing, even for me.

—Andy Grove, Chairman of Intel

A retired member of the U.S. intelligence community once told me that one of the original reasons why the government subsidized the agricultural industry was so that we would be able to produce all of our own food in the event of military hostilities. If World War III breaks out, and we can't rely on nations that we have during peacetime, the survival of the U.S. will depend upon our ability to grow our own food, build our own weapons, and manufacture our own medicine.

There is no doubt that sustaining technical leadership is a matter of national security. As offshore outsourcing grows as a trend, our risk of losing superiority will increase. If our high-tech corporations become dependent upon foreign labor to do their R&D, which many companies have already sent offshore, then we will be in a *world of hurt* if hostilities break out.

The sad truth is that profits often matter more to corporations than national security. For example, high-powered computers are used to simulate nuclear explosions. Both the Russians and Chinese have sought to illegally obtain the necessary hardware from the U.S. to do so. The Federation of American Scientists reports that on July 31, 1998, IBM was fined $8.5 million for exporting computers to a Russian nuclear laboratory.[51] In 1996, Silicon Graphics sold computers to a Russian nuclear laboratory (Chelyabinsk-70, located in Snezhinsk) in violation of export laws. SGI paid $182,000 in civil fines and $1 million in criminal fines.[52] In 2003, Sun Microsystems was found guilty of exporting high-powered computing equipment to China and was fined $291,000.[53]

---

51 `http://www.fas.org/nuke/control/export/news/980731-doj.htm`

52 *"Sun fined for illegally exporting computers to China,"* Associated Press *(December 16, 2003)*

53 *Ibid.*

Closing Remarks

If upper management is worth a damn, it won't offshore merely because it seems like the thing to do. Successful offshore outsourcing necessitates a solid business case, one that spells out well-defined benefits. When it comes down to it, offshoring isn't an end in itself—which is to say that it won't save a company that's already headed downhill.

The companies that successfully utilize offshore outsourcing will be the same companies that already have their act together. These are the corporations that know how to institute processes necessary to protect their mission-critical projects from the type of amateurish shenanigans that occur in the minor leagues. In other words, if a company can't properly execute its other business tasks, then offshore outsourcing will likely aggravate things.

CHAPTER 4

Arguments in Favor of Offshoring

Chapter at a Glance

Where do you want to go today?

—Old Microsoft Slogan

Pick something to move offshore today.

—Senior Vice President Brian Valentine

While you read this chapter, keep in mind that this isn't Reverend Blunden speaking (I'll return in the following chapter, with a vengeance). The voice that I'm assuming in this chapter is an amalgam of public relations specialists, industry pundits, media talking heads, think-tank "experts," management consultants, and chief executives. In this chapter, I'm going to outline the arguments that these people use to support the idea of offshore outsourcing. If you've read the *Wall Street Journal*, watched *Fox News*, or flipped through a magazine like *The Economist*, you will, no doubt, have already come across this chapter's candy-coated apologies. Offshore outsourcing is referred to as a "win-win" formula, and CEOs claim that they need to "choose to compete."

Go ahead and chew on those sound bites, if you wish—just don't swallow. If you happen to make this mistake, call 1-800-222-1222 to find out where your local Poison Control Center is.

NOTE To be frank, it sickens me to have to echo the sympathies of someone like Carly Fiorina or Brian Valentine. Nevertheless, my publisher has requested that I present an even-handed approach to this topic and that's, ahem, what I'm going to try and do.

The people who support offshoring claim that the cost savings which result from offshoring will ultimately benefit the general American public. They claim that displaced workers will find better jobs and usher in the next wave of innovation. Furthermore, offshoring proponents claim that the coming labor shortage, coupled with competitive forces, leave them no alternative but to go offshore. The best solution is to sit back and let the free market do its thing. Hand everything over to Adam Smith and his invisible hand.

How Companies Benefit

Companies are merely replicating what they do at home, where labor is expensive and capital is relatively cheap, in countries in which the reverse is true.

—*The McKinsey Quarterly* no. 4, 2003

The immediate benefactors of offshoring are large multinational corporations. Having access to cheap labor overseas, according to advocates, provides benefits like

- Reduced costs
- More efficient allocation of resources
- Increased productivity
- Additional revenue
- Repatriated earnings
- Reduced turnover
- Increased flexibility
- Disaster recovery

Reduced Costs

Cost savings are the fundamental advantage of offshoring—which is to say that cost savings (hypothetically) give rise to all the other benefits. If companies couldn't save money, they wouldn't go overseas. The other advantages afforded by offshore outsourcing are conditionally dependent on this one.

Cost savings are a consequence of the differential between salaries at home and abroad. As mentioned in Chapter 1, the Bureau of Labor Statistics (BLS) reports that the average IT salary in the U.S. was $61,630 in 2002. A top-shelf engineering graduate from the Indian Institute of Technology (IITS) only costs $10,000 per year.[1] Considering the average salary of an IT worker in India starts at around $5,880, the savings will probably being even greater than that.[2]

The McKinsey Global Institute (MGI), a research group within McKinsey & Company, asserts that every dollar spent offshore results in a net savings of 58 cents.[3] MGI also claims that savings of up to 65 to 70 percent of initial costs can be achieved if an offshoring project is judiciously implemented.[4]

More Efficient Allocation of Resources

Imagine having to build your own car when you needed one. Before Henry Ford introduced the assembly line, this is what a lot of people actually did. It was time-consuming and expensive, and the parts weren't standardized.

---

[1] *Manjeet Kripalani and Pete Engardio, "The Rise of India,"* Business Week *(December 8, 2003)*

[2] *Stephanie Overby, "A Buyer's Guide to Offshore Outsourcing,"* CIO Magazine *(November 15, 2002)*

[3] *McKinsey Global Institute, "Offshoring, Is It a Win-Win Game?" (August 2003)*

[4] *Ibid.*

Offshore outsourcing allows companies to focus on their core competencies, spending resources only in areas where they have strategic assets and relegating everything else to an external service provider.

Instead of building a car yourself, you go to a dealership. Instead of managing your own call center, you farm it out to an offshore provider. As with a car dealership, offshore service providers, due to special expertise or lower cost structure, can offer a comparable product (if not a superior product) for a much lower price.

Increased Productivity

According to Diana Farrell, director of the McKinsey Global Institute

> *There is an assumption by protectionists that these jobs are going somewhere else, and all this money has been pocketed by CEOs who take it home. A little more sophisticated version is: It's being pocketed by companies in the form of profits. One step further and you say those profits are either going to go as returns to the investors in those companies, or they're going to go into new investment by those companies.*[5]

Hence, cost savings from offshore operations can be

- Channeled to investors
- Reinvested

While the first option doesn't lead to increased productivity, the second one can. Money saved from sending work offshore can be used to fund research and development—research and development that a company might not normally be able to afford. Competition during the market downturn has forced companies to cut back on core R&D. In 2002, it's reported that research and development spending by public U.S. companies fell 2 percent.[6] There are some analysts who claim that a well-engineered offshore operation can generate enough cost savings to add an additional 20 percent to a company's R&D budget.[7]

The more research and development a company performs, the more opportunity the company has to innovate. The more a company innovates, the more productive it can become, and the more benefits are passed down as lower prices. Lower software and hardware prices will encourage businesses to

---

[5] *Ericka Kinetz, "Who Wins and Who Loses as Jobs Move Overseas?,"* New York Times *(December 7, 2003)*

[6] *George Gilbert and Rahul Sood, "Outsourcing's Offshore Myth,"* CNET News.com *(December 15, 2003,* `http://news.com.com/2010-1022_3-5121783.html`*)*

[7] *Ibid.*

implement new IT systems. This is important because companies that invest in new IT systems tend to be more productive themselves, such that the increase in productivity is twofold. Research done at the New York Federal Reserve demonstrated that "those industries that made the largest IT investments in the early 1990s show larger productivity gains in the late 1990s."[8]

For example, Texas Instruments has a chip design operation in Bangalore. The company employs approximately 900 engineers at this location, and the core R&D that the Bangalore facility executes has produced 225 patents.[9] Going offshore has allowed Texas Instruments to leverage the pool of cheap labor and spur innovation.

Cummins, an American company headquartered in Indiana, manufactures service engines. The company has set up an R&D facility in the Indian city of Pune. According to Steve Chapman, the company's international vice president, Cummins will be able to use its existing $250 million budget "to introduce five or six new engines a year instead of two."[10]

One thing that the people at MGI also pointed out was that people in India have a different perspective of call center and back-office operations. Jobs that Americans would look down on as being menial low-level work are sought-after in India. Let's face it—when you live in a country where a quarter of the population is below the poverty line, almost half of the people are illiterate, and malnutrition is a serious threat, any job is a good job.[11] Thus, Indians are more grateful for their work, and they tend to work harder, and this results in high productivity.

NOTE Employers like desperation. Desperation translates into fear, which makes people work harder. As we all know, a comfortable employee never works as hard as a desperate one. There's nothing like a little abject terror to raise productivity levels.

Another reason why offshoring raises productivity levels is that the cheap labor can be used to do things that would be prohibitively expensive in the U.S., like build in-house software solutions or chase down delinquent credit card accounts.

Cheaper labor also boosts productivity by facilitating round-the-clock software development. As I mentioned in Chapter 2, Oracle is looking to double the number of workers at its seven-acre Hyderabad campus to 6,000 in an effort to support shift-based software development.[12] This is in line with Larry's sober vision of the software industry, in which application development

---

[8] *Kevin J. Stiroh,* Information Technology and the U.S. Productivity Revival: What Do the Industry Data Say? *Federal Reserve Bank of New York (January 24, 2001)*

[9] *Manjeet Kripalani and Pete Engardio, "The Rise of India,"* BusinessWeek *(December 8, 2003)*

[10] *Ibid.*

[11] *Central Intelligence Agency,* World Fact Book 2003 *(Brasseys, Inc., 2003)*

[12] *Aaron Davis, "Software Developers Calling Shots,"* Mercury News *(November 9, 2003)*

projects will eventually resemble the factories of the manufacturing industry. Like a steel mill, programmers will work in shifts. Engineers arriving at work in the morning will pick up where their evening-shift peers left off, resulting in a nonstop production process.

Additional Revenue

Outsourcing in other countries produces an increase in demand for goods and services in the U.S. Setting up an offshore operation requires telecommunication equipment, networking hardware, high-end servers, desktop computers, and software. Most of these products are bought from companies based in the U.S. The same goes for legal and marketing services based in the U.S.

MGI claims that for every dollar that is invested overseas, offshore operations purchase five cents worth of goods from the U.S. economy.[13] According to data provided by the U.S. Government Export Portal,[14] in 1992 the U.S. exported $1.9 billion of merchandise to India. Ten years later, in 2002, the U.S. exported $4 billion dollars of merchandise to India.

Repatriated Earnings

Because large multinational companies like IBM, GE, and Intel are incorporated in the U.S., their earnings are repatriated back home. This manifests itself primarily in terms of shareholder value (assuming that the shareholders are American).

MGI claims that for every dollar that is invested overseas, offshore operations repatriate four cents back to the U.S.[15]

Reduced Turnover

With respect to white collar knowledge-based jobs, turnover is expensive. Software architects, insurance risk assessors, and research scientists must climb a significant learning curve. Climbing this curve can take anywhere from eight months to eight years. When a high-level employee leaves, all of the knowledge and experience that they've accumulated goes right out the door with them, and the employer must invest the resources necessary to regrow that expertise. If enough people like this leave, a company can go under.

Every company has a *truck number*. The truck number metric is determined by calculating how many people you'd have to run over with a truck to disable a company. This type of information is valuable. An unscrupulous corporation could potentially destroy a competitor by buying off these people

---

[13] *McKinsey Global Institute, "Offshoring, Is It a Win-Win Game?" (August 2003)*

[14] `http://www.export.gov/tradestatistics.html`

[15] *McKinsey Global Institute, "Offshoring, Is It a Win-Win Game?" (August 2003)*

or sabotaging their work. In the wrong hands, a truck number list could be devastating. If the truck number people leave, it spells certain doom for everyone else.

The problem of turnover was one reason why Allstate Insurance moved part of its operations offshore. In 1999, due to heavy turnover and mounting salaries, Allstate moved one of its IT operations to Northern Ireland. The company now employs 650 people there.[16] According to Mike Scardino, assistant vice president for finance, "We had an additional issue in that we had a large number of contractors working for us here in Chicago, and they were extremely expensive. With the labor crunch and Y2k, we had a ratio of 50 percent contractors who were constantly leaving for higher-paying jobs."[17]

Increased Flexibility

Hiring new employees is a labor-intensive process. There's the initial phone interview, the face-to-face interview, the follow-up interview (if necessary), and the time spent on negotiating a compensation package. All told, scheduling the whole process and weighing the alternatives can take months.

The same sort of problem exists with respect to the means of production. Factories take years to build and can cost hundreds of millions of dollars. AMD, for example, will spend the next four years and $2.4 billion dollars to build a fabrication plant named AMD Fab 36.[18] AMD's new facility will produce semiconductors whose design rule is on the order of 65 nanometers.

When demand exceeds production capacity, most businesses don't have the resources to hire the necessary manpower or build new manufacturing facilities. For example, Apple, which shipped 787,000 Macintosh computers in the fourth quarter of 2003,[19] would probably be hard pressed if it suddenly got an urgent order for 200 million Macintosh computers.

This is why offshoring service-based work is attractive to companies that suddenly need to scale. Rather than overburden their own HR staff or make hurried investments in capital equipment, companies can relegate work to an offshore service provider. Large providers, like TCS and Wipro, have the labor pool and facilities required to handle tasks that abruptly grow in size.

Disaster Recovery

We live in an uncertain world. Back in August 2001, if you told somebody that you were concerned about terrorists dive-bombing the World Trade

---

[16] *Steve Ulfelder, "Ireland: Comfort and Convenience at a Higher Cost,"* Computerworld *(September 15, 2003)*

[17] *Julia King, "The Best of Both Shores: Outsourcing Watch 2003,"* Computerworld *(April 21, 2003)*

[18] *John G. Spooner, "AMD Breaks Ground on New Chip Plant,"* CNET News.com *(November 20, 2003,* `http://marketwatch-cnet.com.com/2100-1006_3-5109686.html`*)*

[19] `http://www.apple.com/pr/library/2003/oct/15results.html`

Center, they probably would have called you a paranoid freak. Paranoid or not, Computer Economics estimated that it will cost $15.8 billion to rebuild the IT infrastructure destroyed in the World Trade Center collapse.[20] According to David Johnson of AT&T, "The square mile surrounding the World Trade Center is without doubt the most intensive square mile of telecom on Planet Earth."[21]

Having facilities offshore is a way to help ensure continuity of business in the event of a disaster. Most remote backup locations only require some office space and a custodial IT staff. The availability of cheap labor and land in places like India allows contingency plans to be implemented at a very low cost.

Job Losses Are No Big Deal

Any job losses must be seen as part of an ongoing process of economic restructuring, with which the U.S. economy is well acquainted.

—*The McKinsey Quarterly* no. 4, 2003

Forrester's prediction of 3.3 million jobs going offshore by 2015 may sound dire, but it needs to be put in perspective. This number may seem awe inspiring until it's viewed within a larger context. For example, the Bureau of Labor Statistics reports, in its *Current Population Survey*, that from "[the] January 1999 through December 2001 period, 4.0 million workers were displaced from jobs they had held for at least 3 years."

The BLS also records "mass layoff statistics." Specifically, the BLS tracks an *extended mass layoff* statistic, which (according to the BLS) represents "layoffs in establishments that have at least 50 initial claims filed against them during a 5-week period and where the employer indicates that 50 or more people were separated from their jobs for at least 31 days." In other words, the BLS is tracking people who lost their jobs and haven't been able to find one for a significant amount of time.

Table 4-1 displays the number of extended mass layoff claimants in the private industry from 1996 to 2002. Forrester's figure of 3.3 million jobs over the next 12 years works out to about 275,000 jobs per year. In 1999, mass layoffs accounted for more than three times this number.

---

[20] *Clint Boulton, "IT Infrastructure Re-Building Will Top $15 Billion,"* Internetnews.com *(September 14, 2001,* `http://www.internetnews.com/infra/article.php/10693_884901`*)*

[21] *Thomas Armistead, "Disaster Spawned Opportunity to Vastly Improve Utilities in Area,"* McGraw Hill Construction ENR *(September 9, 2002)*

Table 4-1 Layoffs in the Private Industry 1996–2002

Year	Total Claimants
1996	900,821
1997	989,952
1998	1,179,439
1999	931,272
2000	974,104
2001	1,568,608
2002	1,314,845

Job displacement due to offshoring is just a normal part of the economic ebb and flow of our economy. Offshoring is just like any other factor that attributes to job displacement: technological innovation, changes in regulatory laws, economic downturns, corporate restructuring, and global trade policies.

Even if more than 3.3 million jobs leave the U.S., there's still an upper limit to how many jobs can leave. Roughly 70 percent of the U.S. economy is based on services that are geographically anchored to the country (e.g., personal healthcare, restaurants, retail stores, entertainment).[22] These are jobs that can't be taken offshore.

The Job Ladder

To be competitive and to maintain and improve American living standards, we have to move up the technology food chain.
—Craig R. Barrett, *New York Times*, December 22, 2003

Over the long run, symbolic analysts will do just fine, as long as they stay away from job functions that are becoming routinized [sic].
—Robert B. Reich, *Wall Street Journal*, December 26, 2003

Low-skill jobs like coding are moving offshore and what's left in their place are more advanced project management jobs.
—M. Eric Johnson, *New York Times*, December 7, 2003

Chief executives like Craig Barrett (of Intel) and professors like Robert Reich (former U.S. labor secretary) think that job losses due to offshoring are

[22] *McKinsey Global Institute, "Offshoring, Is It a Win-Win Game?" (August 2003)*

acceptable, even desirable, because it's just a part of economic evolution. We're climbing the job ladder, and in order to climb to the next rung, we need to relegate the current rung to people overseas so that we can focus on more important tasks.

Analogies: The Industrial Revolution

In the years immediately following the "Treaty of Paris" (1783), where England formally recognized the U.S. as a sovereign nation, America was an agrarian society. The country's first president, George Washington, was a farmer who owned several thousand acres of land in Mount Vernon, Virginia.

During the time period leading up to the Civil War, the country began to industrialize as technology spread from England. The decision makers in England knew that their head start with regard to industrialization provided them with an advantage, and they passed laws prohibiting the export of manufacturing equipment.[23] Obviously they failed. Industrialization was inevitable and irreversible. Pandora's box had been opened.

As industrialization progressed, and technology allowed people to become more productive, fewer and fewer people were needed to grow food. According to the Bureau of Labor Statistics *Employment Situation Summary* for December 2003, there are 907,000 people who work in farming, fishing, and forestry occupations. This represents less than 1 percent of the 147 million people employed in the U.S. People who might once have been stuck with tedious farm work now have more interesting jobs in the services sector.

NOTE Of course, industrialization wasn't entirely a bed of roses. It brought other things too, like industrial slums, hazardous working conditions, and child labor. Industrialization also ushered in "robber barons" like John D. Rockefeller, William Vanderbilt, and Jay Gould. These problems were addressed only after several decades of struggle by the labor movement in conjunction with antitrust judgments by the U.S. Supreme Court.

Moving to the Next Rung

Proponents of offshoring, like Robert Reich, claim that the same type of evolution is going on now. Tedious jobs that can be standardized are being sent offshore. The current job rung is being exported to places like India and China so that workers in the U.S. can climb up to the next rung on the ladder.

This next wave of jobs, which Reich refers to as *symbolic analytic work*, will involve high-level creative work and require a college degree.[24] The symbolic analytic category of work includes jobs like R&D, product development,

---

[23] *Carroll W. Pursell,* The Machine in America: A Social History of Technology *(Johns Hopkins University Press, 1995)*

[24] *Robert B. Reich, "Nice Work If You Can Get It,"* Wall Street Journal *(December 26, 2003)*

and design. No other nation on the world does as good a job at preparing its students for this type of work. When the next rung begins to appear, the U.S. will be there to take advantage of it and Americans will, on the whole, benefit.

Therefore, we shouldn't be worried about temporarily losing jobs. Like the farmers of yore, we should embrace improvements in technology and productivity because they offer us a better way of life.

As Robert McTeer Jr., CEO of the Federal Reserve Bank of Dallas, put it, "If you want jobs for jobs' sake, trade in bulldozers for shovels. If that doesn't create enough jobs, replace shovels with spoons."[25]

Adapting: Who Moved My Cheese?

So the jobs are leaving, and there's no sense in fighting it. What do we do?

We have to adapt and survive.

This is the moral of a book, written by Dr. Spencer Johnson, entitled *Who Moved My Cheese?* In this book, four characters are described: two mice (named *Sniff* and *Scurry*) and two mouse-sized humans (*Hem* and *Haw*). All four characters live in a maze and eat cheese. Although the Cheese that Hem and Haw eat is metaphorical (it's whatever makes you happy), and thus denoted by a capital first letter (i.e., Cheese).

As the story unfolds, Hem and Haw become fat and lazy after surviving for quite some time on a particular supply of Cheese. When the Cheese finally disappears, Hem and Haw are dumbfounded. They had become so accustomed to simply eating the Cheese that they felt entitled to it. Hem, in particular, prefers to angrily insist that it isn't fair, that the Cheese will come back because he deserves it.

The mice, Sniff and Scurry, working on instinct, don't notice much of a difference. They look for cheese every day, and so the disappearance isn't much of a shock for them. In other words, Sniff and Scurry are in "survival mode" all the time.

Haw decides to break out of his old ways and try to look for new Cheese. He concludes that change is a natural part of life, and you should constantly keep an eye out for it so that you can preemptively adapt to it. Once more, adapting to change can lead to new Cheese, which tastes just as good, if not better than, the old Cheese.

See? Change isn't so bad.

People who've been displaced by offshoring need to find new Cheese. Stop bitching and start looking. They need to accept what's going on as part of the natural order of things and go with the flow. They need to abandon the stale, old Cheese and find new Cheese. This means acquiring a new skill set and moving up the food chain towards jobs that create more value.

The bottom line: in a global labor market, work will gravitate to wherever it can be done most cheaply. You can sit and ignore reality, or you can embrace it and grow. Offshoring isn't a zero-sum game. It can be a win-win scenario.

---

[25] *Robert D. McTeer, "The Dismal Science? Hardly!"* Wall Street Journal *(June 4, 2003)*

Poverty-stricken people in other countries get a chance at a better life, and American workers get to assume more fulfilling occupations.

The Labor Shortage

> *People focus oftentimes on the labor rate differential. But the thing that's most troubling is the graduation rate of technical graduates.*
>
> —Steve Ballmer, CEO Microsoft, *Bloomberg News*, December 23, 2003

One of the reasons for raising the cap on the H-1B program in 2000, and for offshore outsourcing, is the shortage of American engineers. According to the Census Bureau's *National Population Estimate* for October 2003, there were 291 million people living in the U.S. The Census Bureau also projects that the U.S. population in 2010 will be around 300 million. Table 4-2 offers an age breakdown for the U.S. population in 2002 and 2010.

The age breakdown of the 2002 data set is given by the Census Bureau's *Population Estimate—Characteristics* chart that looked at age and sex. The age breakdown for the year 2010 is given by the Census Bureau's *Projections of the Total Resident Population* report (see Census Bureau data set NP-T3).

Table 4-2 Age Breakdown of U.S. Population

Age	2002	2010
Under 5 years	19,609,147	20,099,000
5 to 9 years	19,900,837	19,438,000
10 to 14 years	21,136,449	19,908,000
15 to 19 years	20,376,151	21,668,000
20 to 24 years	20,213,631	21,151,000
25 to 29 years	18,971,891	19,849,000
30 to 34 years	20,956,412	19,002,000
35 to 39 years	21,914,882	19,039,000
40 to 44 years	23,001,724	20,404,000
45 to 49 years	21,302,064	22,227,000
50 to 54 years	18,781,873	21,934,000
55 to 59 years	14,990,542	19,177,000
60 to 64 years	11,611,184	16,252,000
65 to 69 years	9,580,927	12,159,000
70 to 74 years	8,693,288	8,995,000

Age	2002	2010
75 to 79 years	7,420,394	7,175,000
80 to 84 years	5,314,239	5,600,000
85 to 89 years	2,942,567	3,476,000
90 to 94 years	1,249,983	1,625,000
95 to 99 years	341,829	556,000
100 years and over	58,684	129,000

Assuming that the working population lies between the ages of 20 and 55, Table 4-3 specifies the percentage of the population in 2002 and 2010 that lies in this age range. The net effect will be a 2 percent decrease in the relative size of the working population.

Table 4-3 Age Breakdown of Working Population

Range	2002	2010
0 to 19 years	28	27
20 to 54 years	50	48
55 to 100 years	22	25

According to the Bureau of Labor Statistics, there were 147 million civilian jobs available in December 2003. The BLS *Employment Projection* study forecasts that the number of jobs in 2010 will be 168 million. This is 20 million greater than the working population of 2015 (144 million, 48 percent of 300 million). The only way to deal with this shortage is to rely on offshore labor.

The shortage of graduates who have majored in mathematics and science will be particularly severe. Craig Barrett, Chief Executive at Intel (a company that is aggressively hiring offshore) claims that Intel can't find enough talent locally to satisfy their hiring needs.[26] The National Center for Education Statistics reports in its 2002 *Digest of Education Statistics* (Table 265) that only 58,098 of the 1.24 million students who received bachelor degrees in 2001 were in engineering. That's less than 5 percent. It's interesting to note that topping the list were social sciences (128,036) and business (265,746).

[26] *"Relocating the Back Office,"* The Economist *(December 11, 2003)*

The Free Market

The time's long gone when we could assume there was a God-given right to an American job. Protectionism will only make things worse.

—Charles Cooper, Executive Editor, *CNET News.com*

Today we face a choice: Do we compete or retreat?

—Computer Systems Policy Project (CSPP), *Choose to Compete*

Outsourcing is just a new way of doing international trade. . . . More things are tradable than were tradable in the past. And that's a good thing.

—N. Gregory Mankiw, chairman of Bush's Council of Economic Advisors

A *free market economy* is one in which buyers and sellers are allowed to engage in exchange, based on prices that are reached through mutual agreement, in the absence of government intervention. In other words, it is an economy whose markets are free from external coercion by a political body. In practice, free market advocates seek to minimize government intervention rather than eliminate it entirely. The government, by the way, has a number of techniques that it can use to interfere with the free market, including tariffs, taxes, subsidies, regulation, and flat-out ownership.

Under the free market system, sellers are encouraged to compete for buyers. This is a nice way of saying that it's every man for himself, and let the Devil take the hindmost. Companies are free to pursue their own best interests within the confines of the law (and sometimes that doesn't even stop them). In other words, the implicit aim of any for-profit institution is to dominate its market, maximize its revenue stream, and drive its competitors out of business. Larry Ellison once summarized this as "It's not enough we (Oracle) win, everyone else must lose."[27]

This isn't necessarily a bad thing. Competition benefits consumers by keeping the price of goods and services low. Competition also spurs innovation, which leads to increases in productivity and, ultimately, economic growth. Thus, private vice leads to public good over the long run. At least, that's the way Adam Smith described it in his 1776 book *An Inquiry into the Nature and Causes of the Wealth of Nations*.

Proponents of offshoring believe that the government should stand at the sidelines and let the free market take care of things. U.S. corporations need the resulting competition to keep them on their toes. If the U.S. government institutes protectionist measures, U.S. corporations will become complacent like Hem and Haw. The dearth of competitive forces will allow businesses in the U.S. to keep prices high. Not only that, but government intervention will

---

27 *Karen Southwick,* Everyone Else Must Fail: The Unvarnished Truth About Oracle and Larry Ellison *(Crown Business, 2003)*

permit American corporations to survive without having to innovate. Some people argue that this is what debilitated our steel industry during the 1980s. While Japan was investing in new equipment and more efficient processes, American steel corporations were lobbying for more protection.

In the end, American corporations really don't have a choice. Survival will necessitate offshoring. As long as offshoring is legal, the corporations that offshore will achieve a unique operational disadvantage and put their competition out of business. Either you offshore, or you perish. Pandora's Box has been opened, and there's no way to close it. Rather than wait for the competition to get a head start on the learning curve, U.S. corporations like IBM, Microsoft, and Intel have chosen to dive headfirst into the fad so that they're not left behind.

This reminds me of the *CPU Wars* comic strip[28] in which a drone-like executive at IPM yells out, "If we don't do it, somebody else will!" The IPM automatons, seated around a long conference table, slam their collective fist down and say, "Right you are JT!"

---

[28] `http://www.e-pix.com/CPUWARS/cpuwars.html`

CHAPTER

5

Arguments Against Offshoring

Chapter at a Glance

- ► Manufactured Consent
- ► Cost Savings Aren't Everything
  - ► The Distribution of Wealth in the United States
  - ► Cui Bono?
  - ► $6000 Curtains
  - ► Cost Structure and Head Counts
- ► The Myth of the Job Ladder
  - ► The Cost of Redeployment
  - ► Cheaper Alternatives for the Next Rung
  - ► The Next Big Thing May Occur Offshore
  - ► Who Cut The Cheese?
- ► Job Losses Are a Big Deal
- ► The Myth of the Labor Shortage
  - ► Age Discrimination
  - ► Skill Set Hypocrisy
  - ► The Retention Problem
  - ► Not Enough Engineers
  - ► The Self-Fulfilling Prophesy
- ► The Myth of the Free Market
- ► The Fundamental Issue
- ► End Game
- ► What Can I Possibly Do?

In the previous chapter, I examined the various arguments that Corporate America, in its numerous guises, uses to justify offshore outsourcing. I'll admit that I had ulterior motives aside from just trying to be evenhanded. Like a stack of wooden blocks, I carefully built up the conceptual framework of offshoring proponents just so I could knock it back down. In the pages that follow, I'll address each pro-offshoring argument in turn, chopping away at its underpinnings until it collapses under the force of its own shortcomings.

The American multinationals probably went to a lot of trouble and spent a lot of money to come up with positive ways to spin offshoring. They hired PR specialists, they brainstormed with marketing consultants, they formed industry organizations, and they funded researchers at think tanks to write studies; anything to keep them from looking like a bunch of two-bit sellouts.

Liars and Leaders

As it turns out, what makes people effective communicators also makes them convincing liars. Which is a nice way of saying that a lot of the political and business leaders in the world are con artists. In a 1994 study performed by Dr. Caroline Keating, a professor at Colgate University, Keating found that males who excelled in deception also emerged as leaders in their peer groups.[1] This is something to bear in mind while reading an annual report or when voting during an election.

Rick Chapman, author of *In Search of Stupidity*,[2] relates one of my favorite examples. A couple of decades ago, two consultants from McKinsey & Co., Tom Peters and Robert Waterman, wrote a nifty piece of propaganda called *In Search of Excellence*. It was a smash hit, and garnered a cult-like following. It was discovered later on, however, that Peters faked the data that the book based its conclusions on. According to Peters, "This is pretty small beer, but for what it's worth, okay, I faked the data."[3]

Wait a minute! Let me get this straight, a couple of guys from the country's most prestigious strategic consulting firm flat-out fudged their numbers? Small beer? Excuse me, but aren't McKinsey consultants supposed to be honest? I thought that outright lying was the domain of shyster attorneys and used-car salesman? Do you suppose that this might bring other studies done by McKinsey employees under scrutiny (ahem, "Offshoring: Is it a Win-Win Game")? Do you think that, like Peters and Waterman, they might have a vested interest in exercising a little creative license?

---

[1] *C. F. Keating and K. R. Heltman, "Dominance and Deception in Children and Adults: Are Leaders the Best Misleaders?"* Personality and Social Psychology Bulletin *20 (1994): pp. 312–321.*

[2] *Merrill R. Chapman,* In Search of Stupidity *(Apress, 2003)*

[3] *John A. Byrne, "The Real Confessions of Tom Peters,"* BusinessWeek *(December 3, 2001,* `http://www.businessweek.com/magazine/content/01_49/b3760040.htm`*)*

They furtively hope to redirect your attention away from what they're doing. It's called slight of hand, folks—now you see it, now you don't. Poof, your job is gone. Harry Blackstone Jr. would be proud.

In my mind, the conceptual framework used by offshoring proponents is nothing more than a convenient ideological weapon that the business elite uses to pursue their own best interests. It's propaganda dressed up in evening wear and delivered by smartly dressed front men. It's an attempt to establish a business case for class warfare.

In this chapter, I have regained control of my voice and have instituted a zero idiot tolerance. In this chapter, the misconceptions and half-truths of the previous chapter will be shot on sight. The corporate aristocrats, with their juicy compensation packages and their shiny executive crowns, will be flushed out into the open, naked for all to see.

Can your see the smoke rising, off in the distance?

Can you smell the cordite?

Can you hear the low metallic "click" of a safety being released?

Those double-talkers have foolishly wandered into my Area of Operation.

Reverend Blunden is about to open fire.

Manufactured Consent

If you've been keeping abreast of offshoring in the news, you've no doubt heard one or more pro-offshoring arguments in various permutations. At first glance, they seem to be very convincing, especially the ones that use historical analogies. After all, the industrial revolution and the service revolution that followed it did provide American workers with the opportunity to escape factory jobs for knowledge-based positions. Our competitive economic system does spur innovation. Disturbing the integrity of our free market system would be a bad idea, wouldn't it?

What the pro-offshoring doctrine seems to say is that to obstruct offshore outsourcing is to impede innovation and progress. Intervention would prevent us from satisfying the labor demands of our growing economy and allow American industries to lose their competitive edge. Innovation, progress, the free market: all these concepts seem to be good things, things that any well-intentioned person wouldn't want to challenge. This, my dear reader, is exactly what the corporate advocates want. This is their little trap. The corporations want to assume the high ground, such that anyone challenging them must appear to be in the wrong (read un-American).

Not many people have challenged the corporate stance. However, this hasn't been because they were worried about looking un-American. People haven't critically dissected the offshoring doctrine of free markets and job evolution because the media has been exercising its most powerful weapon: silence.

The pro-offshoring arguments are pretty much all that you see in the news. The media may once in a while give voice to a disgruntled IT worker whose job has been exported to India, but that's it. They might offer a quote or two about how badly life sucks for IT people ("Boy, I hate it when American corporations do that!"), but the media never goes any deeper than this. *None of the pro-offshoring arguments, or their underlying assumptions, is scrutinized with any degree of rigor.* Is it surprising that the very key to debunking the pro-offshoring position depends upon the ability of the audience to do just that? To see beyond the sound bites, you need to take a closer look and test the veracity of fundamental assumptions.

There's a reason why very few journalists in the media takes this skeptical approach: *the same multinational corporations who are sending jobs offshore are the same customers who are buying advertising space.* For example, how often do you see a 2-page IBM spread in the *Wall Street Journal*? Damn near every day, that's how often! Is it any great revelation that newspapers like the *Wall Street Journal* refrain from voicing opinions that could make their sponsors look bad? Sure, you'll read columns by Robert Reich and Robert McTeer that laud the benefits of the free market, but you'd never, ever, hear the *Wall Street Journal* condemn IBM for sending jobs offshore. Oh no, that might cost the *Wall Street Journal* their IBM account.

Esteemed newspapers like the *Wall Street Journal* are businesses, like any other business (and a profitable one at that). They have a product to sell and a market in which to sell that product. In the case of upscale news sources like the *Wall Street Journal* or the *Economist*, the product consists of readers and the market consists of advertisers.[4] They are essentially selling their readers (an economically privileged audience, i.e., the decision makers) to other large corporations. The advertisers use their spotlight to frame public debate and hold sway over the nation's day-to-day agenda. Given this product-market dynamic, naturally the views put forth will be those that cater to the needs of the corporate sponsors and pander to the wants (or illusions) of the readers. You won't hear a word against offshoring because both groups stand to benefit.

Cost Savings Aren't Everything

That cost savings can be realized from offshore outsourcing isn't up for debate. Obviously, when you farm out work to a country whose GDP per capita is a fraction of that in the U.S., you're going to save money, even if there are various hidden costs associated with communication and remote management. Once the learning curve has been ascended and quality control measures implemented, companies that understand their business processes (i.e., have their act together) will be able to chip away at their overall cost structure. If this weren't the case, multinationals like IBM and HP wouldn't continue to

---

[4] *Noam Chomsky,* Understanding Power *(The New Press, 2002)*

aggressively expand their offshore operations like they are. The fact that many of the companies discussed in Chapter 2 are planning to more than double their offshore presence is testimony to this.

The existence of cost savings however, doesn't necessarily mean that offshoring benefits the average American, or is good for our country in the long run.

The Distribution of Wealth in the United States

In the late 1800s, an Italian economist named Vilfredo Pareto originally stated the *Pareto Principle*, otherwise known as the *80:20 rule*.[5] Pareto discovered that roughly 80 percent of the wealth in Italy was owned by 20 percent of the population. Unfortunately, the state of affairs in the U.S. today is even worse.

Pundits who support offshoring will blithely claim that increases in stock price benefit the average citizen because 50 percent of the U.S. population owns stock.[6] However, the *amount of stock owned* (i.e., concentration of ownership) is really the salient factor, not merely stock ownership in and of itself. Which is to say that owning 100 million shares is different from owning 100 shares.

The *Survey of Consumer Finances* (SCF)[7] is an official survey sponsored every three years by the Board of Governors of the Federal Reserve System. This is probably the most comprehensive and accurate summary of how wealth is distributed here in the states. Recent updates, since 2001, have been reported in the *Federal Reserve Bulletin* 89 (January 2003).

A researcher names James Poterba, an economics professor at MIT, published a paper that used data from the 1998 SCF.[8] According to Poterba, the distribution of assets follows the data provided in Table 5-1.

Table 5-1 Distribution of Assets (2000)

Income	Common Stock	Nonequity Financial Assets	Net Worth
Top 5%	37%	24.2%	25.6%
Next 0.5%	10.7%	7.8%	8.4%
Next 4%	27.2%	26.2%	23.4%
Next 5%	11.3%	14.0%	11.4%

Continued

[5] *Luigino Bruni,* Vilfredo Pareto and the Birth of Modern Microeconomics *(Edward Elgar, 2002)*

[6] *Joint Economic Committee, U.S. Congress,* The Roots of Broadened Stock Ownership *(April 2000)*

[7] `http://www.federalreserve.gov/pubs/oss/oss2/scfindex.html`

[8] *James Poterba, "Stock Market Wealth and Consumption,"* The Journal of Economic Perspectives *14, no. 2 (Spring 2000)*

Table 5-1 *Continued*

Income	Common Stock	Nonequity Financial Assets	Net Worth
Next 10%	9.8%	13.9%	12.8%
Next 80%	4.1%	14%	18.5%

Source: Dr. James Poterba, analysis of SCF data (2000)

What Table 5-1 says is that 20 percent of the U.S. population controls over 80 percent of the country's financial assets.

One might argue that the distribution of wealth may have shifted since Porteba's 2000 study. After all, it has been four years. We're a progressive society—things change, right? Let's look at the 2001 SCF data to get a more recent synopsis. Table 5-2 displays the average net worth (gross assets minus debt) for different income brackets. As you can see, the top income bracket experienced the greatest percentage increase in average net worth, and this would indicate that, if anything, the wealthy members of society have an even greater percentage of the country's total wealth.

Table 5-2 Distribution of Assets (2001)

Percentile of Income	1998	2001 (in Thousands)
Less than 20	52.0	52.6 (1% increase)
20–39.9	104.7	114.3 (9% increase)
40–59.9	137.6	160.9 (17% increase)
60–79.9	223.4	292.1 (31% increase)
80–89.9	354.0	456.5 (30% increase)
90–100	1,684.0	2,258.2 (35% increase)

Source: Federal Reserve Bulletin *(January 2003): Table 3*

Let's look at a specific company, Microsoft. According to Microsoft's 2003 proxy statement,[9] insiders own approximately 15 percent of the company's outstanding shares (i.e., 1,632,652,742 of 10,812,468,881 shares). The ownership summary at *Reuters* online[10] indicates that 1,362 different financial institutions own about 53 percent of Microsoft's shares (i.e., 5,681,114,399). Thus, the big boys own 68 percent of Microsoft's outstanding shares.

[9] `http://www.microsoft.com/msft/SEC/FY03/proxy2003.mspx`

[10] `http://www.investor.reuters.com`

The inescapable fact is that the majority of the wealth (stocks, bonds, real estate, etc.) in this country is controlled by a relatively small group of people who reside at the top of the income spectrum. The average Joe, for all intents and purposes, isn't even on the map. If he is, it's usually on behalf of a 401K plan or a pension.

We don't live in a classless society, do we? Once you've reached this conclusion, understanding the true nature of offshore outsourcing will become easier.

Cui Bono?

Recall in the previous chapter I stated that the cost savings from offshore operations could be

- Channeled to investors
- Reinvested

Even if money is reinvested, it's done so with the long-term intent of increasing the company's value such that the end result is an increase in stock price. The ultimate beneficiaries of a corporation's profits are its owners, the stockholders.

But who are the stockholders? As you can see from the last section, it turns out that the serious players in the stock market are large institutions and the wealthy. Stock price increases due to offshoring won't benefit the people who are affected the most. The Pareto Principle is alive and well. Jumps in stock price resulting from cost savings and innovation don't do anything for those American workers who get thrown overboard for cheaper substitutes offshore. The people whom offshore outsourcing benefits are the same people who own large blocks of stock. My bet is that these people aren't worried about making next month's rent or paying for health insurance.

Thus, when Carly Fiorina talks about benefiting stockholders, she's talking about well-paid executive types like . . . Carly Fiorina. You know, the type of people who can afford to have an entourage of beauticians follow them around.

According to the Federal Reserve's 2001 SCF, the median value for the average annual family income was $39,900.[11] Given Microsoft's price (on February 1, 2004) of $27.40 per share, this would be the equivalent of 1,456 shares of Microsoft stock. This goes to show that even if the stock price shot up by ten points, the real beneficiaries would be the insiders and institutions. The average Joe would probably only make enough money to cover room and board for a few months.

The truth about the stock market is that in order to truly benefit from upward movements in stock price, you have to own thousands, if not millions,

[11] Federal Reserve Bulletin *(January 2003):Table 1, p. 5*

of shares. This means that you have to have money to start with (i.e., it takes money to make money). The only people with this kind of capital on hand are the people at the top of the income spectrum. For instance, in 2003 the IRS reported that the 400 wealthiest taxpayers in the year 2000 had an average income of 174 million.[12] These are the people who can make real money off of the stock market. Not average Joe and his $39,900 a year job—he'll be lucky if he can afford a share or two of Berkshire Hathaway.

$6000 Curtains

By the late '90s . . . CEOs who traveled the high road did not encounter heavy traffic.

—Warren Buffet, 2002 letter to investors

Even if stockholders are in a position to make gains from corporate profits, there's no guarantee that the cost savings produced by offshoring will manifest themselves as an increase in stock price.

In more than a handful of cases, potential shareholder profits have been redirected for the sake of offering executives hefty cash bonuses, suspicious loans, juicy severance packages, and, ahem, reimbursement for "business expenses." All of these extras are paid for courtesy of the stockholder.

In 2001, Merrill Lynch laid off 17,400 people (25 percent of its workforce) and profits declined by 85 percent.[13] This didn't stop the CEO, David Komansky, from receiving a cash bonus of $1 million. According to the *Wall Street Journal*, "The median cash bonus rose 26% to $605,000 for the heads of 69 big companies whose fiscal year ended between Jan. 1 and June 30."[14]

CEO "loans" have also cropped up lately as an executive perk. In 2001, E*TRADE's foul-mouthed chief executive, Christos Cotsakos, was allowed to skip on payment of a $15 million loan that the company extended to him.[15] This was a year in which E*TRADE lost $242 million.

Someone please give that man a bar of soap so he can wash his mouth out.

Adelphia Communications loaned its former boss, John Rigas, $2.3 billion.[16] Gee, I wonder what he was going to use it for? Maybe he wanted to buy his own stealth bomber. WorldCom extended Bernie Ebbers $408 million in loans when he was the company's CEO.[17] Then there's L. Dennis Kozlowski, the

[12] *David Cay Johnson, "Very Richest's Share of Income Grew Even Bigger, Data Show,"* New York Times *(June 26, 2003)*

[13] *Douglas Feiden, "No Losses for Biggest bosses,"* New York Daily News *(November 3, 2002)*

[14] *Joann Lublin, "Executive Pay Keeps Rising, Despite Outcry,"* Wall Street Journal *(October 3, 2003)*

[15] *Scott Herhold, "E*Trade CEO's Pay Angers Investors,"* Mercury News *(May 5, 2002)*

[16] *Peter Dizikes, "Money for Nothing, Massive Executive Loans Haunt Adelphia and WorldCom,"* ABC News *(May 17, 2002)*

[17] *Ibid.*

former CEO of Tyco International Ltd. He borrowed $13.5 million from Tyco to buy a yacht and another $5 million to buy a ring for his wife.[18]

In the wake of the dot-com implosion, an employee with an annual salary of $50,000 received a severance package in the range of $3,850 to $7,700 before taxes.[19] This is nothing compared to what the executives garnered. Executives who got canned in 2001 and 2002 walked away with $16.5 million on average in cash alone.[20] When WorldCom's old CEO, Bernie Ebbers, was given the boot, he walked away in April 2002 with an outrageous severance deal. In addition to a $1.5 million annual stipend (for the rest of his life), he was given free healthcare, life insurance, and 30 hours of travel per year on the WorldCom jet. Thank goodness the WorldCom board came to its senses in September 2002 and rescinded the package.[21]

Finally, there's the old standby: business expenses. L. Dennis Kozlowski redecorated a two-story, 13-room duplex on Fifth Avenue completely with Tyco money. In addition to paying for furnishings, Tyco also covered the bill to put up the seven design consultants who supervised the project. According to an *Associated Press* release, "Kozlowski's lead attorney, Stephen Kaufman, defended the purchases, saying the apartment was listed on Tyco's books as an asset and Kozlowski used it for business purposes."[22]

All told, the project cost Tyco shareholders $18 million. This figure includes a $3.95 million Monet and a $4.7 million Renoir.[23] Hundreds of invoices were submitted to Tyco as a result of the apartment's refurnishing. The list of items purchased for the apartment also includes the following:[24]

$191,250 Persian rug

$125,000 pair of French antique stools

$113,750 George I walnut arabesque clock

$103,000 mirror with gilded wood

$77,000 Ascherberg grand piano

$64,278 pair of Italian armchairs

$38,000 gilt-and-brass backgammon table

$15,000 umbrella stand

---

[18] *Mark Maremont, "Kozlowski's Defense Strategy: Big Spending Was No Secret,"* Wall Street Journal *(February 9, 2004)*

[19] *Rachel Beck, "CEO Severance Deals Seem Bad for Business,"* Associated Press *(March 11, 2003)*

[20] *Ibid.*

[21] *Arianna Huffington,* Pigs at the Trough: How Corporate Greed and Political Corruption Are Undermining America *(Crown, 2003)*

[22] *"Jury to See Lavish Ex-Tyco CEO Lifestyle,"* Associated Press *(December 15, 2003)*

[23] *Arianna Huffington,* Pigs at the Trough: How Corporate Greed and Political Corruption Are Undermining America *(Crown, 2003)*

[24] *Ibid.*

$6,000 shower curtain

$4,995 custom blue-and-gold queen bedskirt

$2,900 set of coat hangers

$2,665 blue velvet custom rectangle pillow

$445 pin cushion

Being the type of man who dotes on his wife, in June 2001 Kozlowski "expensed" half of a $2 million birthday party that he held for his wife in Sardinia.[25] It looks like someone must feel "entitled" to somebody else's money.

Cost Structure and Head Counts

> *When you join a company, you can choose to be a hardworking superstar employee (I don't recommend it) or you can take the Way of the Weasel and accept that you are a head count.*
>
> —Scott Adams, from *The Way of the Weasel*

In addition to its misbegotten fetish for cost structure, management is also obsessed with head count. Head count is important because, in the IT services universe, more warm bodies translate into more billable hours. Not only that, but the more troops that a manager marshals to his call, the more prestige he has. Obviously, a manager with a head count of 200 must be a very important person. As Scott Adams puts it, "As a head count you are essential to supporting the quality of your boss's furniture."

Not only that, but head counts offer a degree of protection. The more bodies you manage, the harder it is for the higher-ups to tear down your little empire. Some devious managers probably hire people just so that they can be sacrificed when things get rough. It's called having a "patsy."

The hope of offshoring is that companies will ultimately be able to do more with less. What the proponents never seem to mention is that they could actually do this without needing to offshore. Rather than throwing everyone overboard for cheaper Indian replacements, why not just hire stellar employees and give them the tools they need to be productive? When it comes to hiring, emphasize quality, not quantity. Get rid of the head counts and keep the first-rate employees. Sure, you can hire six Indian engineers for the price of an American engineer. But if an American engineer can do the work of six Indian engineers, what's the difference? Not only do you get productivity, you get a person who speaks English and who works right down the hall.

[25] *Mark Maremont, "Kozlowski's Defense Strategy: Big Spending Was No Secret,"* Wall Street Journal *(February 9, 2004)*

Why don't corporations take this approach? Well, as PBS writer Robert X. Cringely so aptly put it, "What manager at any big company would trade 100 workers for one, no matter how smart the one? . . . Power and efficiency are in conflict here."[26] In other words, simply relying on a small number of highly productive American employees doesn't lend as much prestige as managing a couple hundred Indian engineers. I mean, who wants to admit, "Uh, yeah, I manage a team of two engineers?"

The Myth of the Job Ladder

The big argument that advocators of offshoring seem to rely upon is the notion that displaced American workers will be able to find more lucrative, higher paying jobs. They claim that outsourcing high-tech jobs will allows American software engineers to go on to more creative, innovative, R&D-type work. In other words, American workers are on a ladder, and outsourcing will allow them to move on to the next rung.

An article by economist Robert Reich in the *Wall Street Journal* (December 26, 2003) proclaims "Technophobes, neo-Luddites, and antiglobalists be warned: You're on the wrong side of history. You see only the loss of old jobs. You're overlooking the new jobs." Predictably, Reich then goes on to talk about how Americans will find work in "R&D, design and engineering."

If it were only back-office and customer contact work that was going offshore, then maybe this argument would have some credibility. *The truth is, however, that a significant percentage of the jobs going offshore are already at the top of the job ladder.* All sorts of knowledge-based and creative work (e.g., R&D, product design, and development) are all being done offshore. I'm not exaggerating either, as people like Jagdish Bhagwati may claim.[27] Over 1,000 patent applications have been filed by American offshore operations in India.[28] Recall some of the information I provided in Chapter 2 and Chapter 4. All the big names are moving top-rung positions overseas. Let's revisit a sample list of the usual suspects.

Microsoft

Microsoft has a Beijing R&D laboratory, where one third of the 180 researchers have their Ph.D.s from American universities. Microsoft will be spending over a billion dollars in India and China in the coming years. Thanks Mr. Gates, nothing like being sold out by one of your own, is there?

---

[26] *Robert X. Cringely, "Body Count: Why Moving to India Won't Really Help IT,"* PBS *(August 7, 2003,* `http://www.pbs.org/cringely/pulpit/pulpit20030807.html`*)*

[27] *Jagdish Bhagwati, "Why Your Job Isn't Moving to Bangalore,"* New York Times *(February 15, 2004)*

[28] *Saritha Rai, "In India, a High-Tech Outpost for U.S. Patents,"* New York Times *(December 15, 2003)*

Intel

Intel's Bangalore campus defines the cutting edge for R&D on the company's 32-bit processors for wireless products and servers. This R&D facility is responsible for 6 of Intel's 60 patent applications in the last 22 months.[29] Intel also has three, count them THREE, large design and development centers in Israel.

HP

HP will also be investing $55 million over the next three years to establish an R&D facility in Singapore to work on networking hardware. Let's hear it for that Singapore Free Trade Agreement!

GE

GE's John Welch Technology Center in India employs 1,800 engineers (450 of which have Ph.D.s). Since 2000, the center has filed for 95 patents.

Motorola

According to Motorola, the company has 16 R&D centers in China, employing over 1,300 R&D engineers (there isn't much of Motorola left in the U.S.). Motorola expects to increase this number to 4,000 by 2006, in addition to spending $1.3 billion on R&D.

Texas Instruments

Texas Instruments has a chip design operation in Bangalore. The company employs approximately 900 engineers at this location, and the core R&D that the Bangalore facility executes has produced 225 patents.

Cisco

Cisco employs 2,500 people in India who perform basic R&D and product development. 500 of those people are full-time Cisco employees, and the rest are outsourced through third-party providers.

Top-Rung Jobs Are Headed Offshore

These large multinational companies are the vanguard. They will set the trend and establish practices that other American businesses will emulate in the near future. U.S. corporations are sending top-rung jobs offshore. The idea that American workers will simply be able to waltz into a new job, higher up on the value food chain, is flawed. It's flawed because of:

---

[29] *Ibid.*

- The cost of redeployment
- Cheaper alternatives for the top rung
- The next big thing may occur offshore
- They didn't move the cheese; they took it away

The Cost of Redeployment

Is it realistic to expect an electrical engineer with 20 years of experience to become a nurse?

—Ron Hira, testimony to House of Representatives, October 20, 2003

The knowledge-based jobs going overseas take years of preparation. Furthermore, specialization has become so acute that moving into a new field essentially requires starting from ground zero. These aren't factory jobs we're talking about that took a couple weeks to learn. Switching from software engineering to biostatistics would require going back to school for four or five years to fill in remedial gaps in the biosciences and complete an advanced degree.

Recall the cost issues that I raised in the Chapter 1. According to the National Center for Education Statistics (NCES), the cost of tuition (and required fees) for graduate school in the 2000–2001 school year was $4,491 per year at a public institution and $15,233 per year at a private institution.[30] This means that the cost floor of a Ph.D. is $17,964. This floor increases to $60,932 at a private university.

To make things interesting, let's assume that your academic record is such that the graduate program you're accepted to provides you a fellowship that covers tuition and offers a monthly stipend of $1,600 *before taxes* (about $20,000 per year pretax). This is the type of award that graduate students are given at Ohio State's Department of Molecular Genetics. In Ohio, this would cover room and board, leaving you with about $500 of expenses to cover per month (e.g., car payment, gas, auto insurance, parking fees, books, etc.). If you took out loans to cover these extra expenses, you'd still end up with $6,000 of debt per year. Obtaining a Ph.D. would cost anywhere from $24,000 to $30,000, and this would be the bare minimum considering that most displaced professionals are mid-career and have other nontrivial expenses (e.g., mortgage, real estate tax, children, etc.).

Let's say that instead of pursuing a degree in the sciences, you decided to go into management. Business school is a whole different can of worms. MBA programs, as a rule, don't offer fellowships like science programs. Most MBA students pay out of their nose and go into debt (i.e., financial aid = student loans). The 2003–2004 tuition and fee costs at a business school like Wharton

---

[30] *U.S. Department of Education, National Center for Education Statistics,* Digest of Education Statistics *(2002):Table 315*

are $37,323. This puts the price tag for an MBA from Wharton at more than $74,646.

If you decide to seek refuge from the IT industry in a creative field, like graphic design or computer animation, you can also expect to crash open your piggy bank. Take the San Francisco Academy of Art College, for example. The cost of tuition and related fees, per semester, is estimated to be in the neighborhood of $7,540. This doesn't include room and board. A two-year associates degree, which usually requires five semesters of effort, will cost you at least $37,700.

Most people I know are still in the process of paying off their first trip to school. Can you imagine a married couple with three children and a house both taking the next two-to-four years off to get new degrees? It's ridiculous! They simply couldn't afford it. Instead of trying to climb to the next rung, they'd both get lower-paying jobs in the service sector. It's a matter of survival, more than anything else. They have bills to pay, and they can't afford to put their lives on hold and return to school.

Finally, let's assume (for the sake of argument) that you do fork over your life savings to go back to school and retool. Who's to say that they won't end up offshoring the job that you train for, or give it to some H-1B Ph.D.? Will you be forced to fund multiple trips back to school, as each job that you train for is sent offshore? Can you imagine the debt that you'd rack up?

What are those offshoring proponents smoking?

Cheaper Alternatives for the Next Rung

It isn't written anywhere that American students have exclusive rights to the next rung on the job ladder. Students from China and India are studying for this next rung at the same time that we are, and often with better results. We don't have a head start in anything anymore; we are neck and neck. If we stumble, they will pull ahead.

Ph.D.s represent the workhorses of corporate R&D. When I spoke with Robert Short, executive VP in charge of Windows Development at Microsoft, he nonchalantly told me that "Usually, we just hire a couple of Ph.D.s from Stanford."

As I mentioned in Chapter 1, The NCES reports that roughly *40–50 percent of the Ph.D.s that graduate in the hard sciences each year are noncitizens*. These are our universities, and in some cases they're churning out as many noncitizen Ph.D.s as American Ph.D.s. They've practically taken over our graduate programs. The fact is that we, as a country, no longer have exclusive domain in any field of research. The idea that American workers will have exclusive ownership of the next big thing is a myth.

Any field that you can go back to school to train in, so can they, and once more they're cheaper. Being cheaper seems to be a big competitive differentiator when it comes to U.S. employers. Foreign Ph.D.s, upon graduating, either return home or try to stay in the U.S. under the H-1B visa program. Either way, they represent a less expensive, but equivalent, substitute.

As Norman Matloff, a computer science professor at U.C. Davis, puts it:

> *Again we see a call for retraining the engineers and programmers. Retraining to do WHAT? This is one of the fundamental myths. These people reason that in past history, when an industry was lost to foreign labor, Americans would have something better to move on to. But key to that was that that new, better thing was something that the foreign workers couldn't do. THIS SITUATION DOES NOT HOLD TODAY. Just what is it that is of a technical nature that these people think won't be done more cheaply by H-1Bs or offshore workers?*

Some people might protest, "Well, maybe this is true in theory . . . " These people aren't aware of the facts. If you don't believe that Matloff is right, you should go back to the list of high-tech companies that I provided in Chapter 2. They're almost all offshoring top-rung jobs of one form or another.

Naturally, one solution to this problem is to place a greater emphasis on the hard sciences (at all levels, K–12 and post-secondary) and to do so in such a way as to give American students a *certifiable advantage* over the flood of foreign students that currently occupy our universities.

In my opinion, most of the political discourse that I've heard about education over the past two decades is just wishful thinking or half-hearted lip service. The last time we truly pushed math and science was in 1957, right after the Soviet Union launched Sputnik. Our leaders were so terrified that the Russians were going to attack us with nuclear weapons from space that they were willing to commit the resources necessary to advance the hard sciences.[31]

This is what it takes to push math and science; you have to threaten our leaders with annihilation. If it doesn't impact them, or their ability to rule, they just don't care.

Alan Tonelson, an economics researcher who wrote *The Race to the Bottom*, has referred to Robert Reich as a supporter of globalization who masquerades as a champion of workers rights.[32] After weighing Reich's "job ladder" theory against facts from the National Center for Education Statistics and the data in Chapter 2, I'm afraid I have to side with Tonelson.

The Next Big Thing May Occur Offshore

Somehow, America has the illusion that it's got a monopoly on innovation, even though the Russians succeeded in launching a satellite before we did and detonated a hydrogen bomb within less than a year of the United State's first H-bomb test. I'll tell you what, if we're so damn innovative, why couldn't we construct the tools necessary to boost productivity, so that we didn't have to outsource offshore to begin with?

---

[31] `http://www.hq.nasa.gov/office/pao/History/sputnik/`

[32] *Alan Tonelson, "High-Tech Jobs: Another Industry Races to the Bottom,"* Tradealert.org *(November 10, 2003)*

American businessmen seem confident that the U.S. will be the exclusive owner of the next big thing, whether it's nanotech or biotech. It's almost as though it's a foregone conclusion. This technological hubris towards the outside world is a dangerous mindset. Andy Grove said it best, "Only the paranoid survive." Those who are confident that they've found the next big thing (thin-client PCs, online grocery stores, micro-kernel database appliances, or web-based application services) usually end up flat on their face, typically after wasting a few hundred million dollars. Like the stock market, nothing's certain in high technology except change.

There is no guarantee that the next big thing will occur in the U.S., and there's no guarantee as to who will benefit or where it will occur. Countries like Japan and China are making headway in nanotech, and there are flourishing biotech R&D centers in Europe. As the deluge of noncitizen Ph.D.s return home from American research universities, this will, no doubt, only serve to strengthen foreign technology programs.

As the number of offshore R&D operations grows, the risk of losing our technical edge will increase. Inevitably, a percentage of the Indian and Chinese scientists will leave to work for local corporations (or the government, depending on their specialty), taking their expertise and mind share with them. U.S. corporations can make their offshore employees sign nondisclosure agreements until they get carpel tunnel, but it won't stop this type of brain drain. As I explained in Chapter 3, intellectual property rights on the international level are almost nonexistent.

Who Cut The Cheese?

This isn't a jobless recovery; it's a job-losing recovery.

—Lester Thurow, economist from MIT, December 12, 2003

The problem with the fable about Hem and Haw, outlined in Chapter 4, is that it naively assumes that there's Cheese somewhere else, and that Hem and Haw are capable of finding it. These rather optimistic assumptions aren't always realistic.

In the case of offshoring, the prohibitive cost of going back to school, coupled with the fact that our system pumps out a tidal wave of noncitizen graduates who are cheaper to hire, makes it difficult to follow the path to the Cheese that people like Robert Reich have mapped out.

Not only that, but also the book mistakenly assumes that change is always for the better. It seems to whisper subliminally, in soothing tones, to the reader that change is always good and can always be relished. "Find the new Cheese and enjoy it."

How about a terminal case of cancer? How about the death of a loved one? How about going to prison? Are Dr. Johnson and his unbridled optimism going to show us the silver lining? Haw can search all he wants, and Hem can defiantly refuse to budge, but both will suffer the same fate: they will both starve to death, because there is no Cheese in this case. It has been taken away.

Job Losses Are a Big Deal

The incomes, the purchasing power of our employees, our workers, our people, are by far more important than what it is we produce.

—Alan Greenspan, in response to a question by Representative Bernard Sanders

Worker redeployment to higher-level jobs is the lynchpin of the pro-offshoring argument. It's the only way that offshoring will ever really lead to a positive outcome. The impact of effective redeployment is the reason why economists like Robert Reich think that job losses are no big deal.

Once this lynchpin is removed, however, the whole shebang comes tumbling down. Given that I've demonstrated that the veracity of this claim is dubious, we can look and see what's really going to happen.

Lori G. Kletzer is a professor of economics at the University of California Santa Cruz. In 2001, the Institute for International Economics published a book by Dr. Kletzer entitled *Job Loss from Imports: Measuring the Costs*. In this book, Kletzer looks at earnings losses suffered by import-competing workers in the manufacturing industry who have been displaced as a result of trade globalization.

From 1979 to 1999, approximately 6.4 million import-competing manufacturing workers were displaced. The study reports that 37 percent of workers surveyed had *not* found a new job. The workers who did find a new job (63 percent of the total) either went into low-paying service positions or returned to manufacturing. The workers who were lucky enough to be reemployed suffered a drop in their average weekly earnings of 13 percent.

What this study says is two things:

- Displaced workers didn't climb the job ladder.
- Displaced workers, on the whole, experienced a drop in income.

When 3.3 million white-collar jobs bite the dust over the next 12 years (and this is a *conservative* estimate according to Forrester's John McCarthy and the Fischer Center's Cynthia Kroll), the same thing will happen. American white-collar workers won't climb the job ladder. If they're lucky, they might find work in their previous field and earn a slightly lower salary. The next rung of innovative positions will go to noncitizen Ph.D.s who graduated from American universities and will do the higher-level jobs for less.

Due to financial pressures (e.g., making mortgage payments, paying for their own health insurance, saving for their own retirement), a nontrivial percentage of displaced American workers will opt for low-paying service jobs in lieu of returning to school, catering to the needs of the corporate elite who sold them out. The average wage of displaced workers in the U.S. will decrease, and this will hurt what Alan Greenspan refers to as their "purchasing power." Essentially, the standard of living for the middle class in the U.S. will take a nosedive.

The fetish for cost structure that corporations have demonstrated will lead them to compete by cutting costs at home. Specifically, companies that don't offshore will be put at a distinct operational disadvantage. To compensate, they will be tempted to cut back on benefits (healthcare, 401K plans) and wages. In order to compete with workers in third-world countries, compensation will be driven down towards third-world levels.

What about innovation?

What about historical analogies?

Didn't the steel industry eventually invest in better equipment and become more productive?

Yes, they did. But my question to you is who benefited? Cui bono? Perhaps a few stockholders made some money, but I doubt if any of the displaced workers owned large blocks of stock. The displaced steel workers experienced a drop in income and a lowering of their standard of living. I grew up in Cleveland during the 1980s; I saw the loss and disillusionment first hand.

Robert Reich's job ladder theory is a crock. "Let them eat cake," he says.

In short, because climbing the job ladder isn't as easy as it sounds, the U.S. will start looking less like a world power, demographically speaking, and more like a third-world country. There will be a small group of corporate elite running the show, and a large group of disenfranchised people living closer to the poverty line.

The Myth of the Labor Shortage

Offshoring proponents in the high-tech industries have claimed that offshoring is necessary because of the shortage of American engineers. This is another myth. The driving force behind multinationals going offshore is cost savings. The truth is that American corporations have created an *artificial* shortage through age discrimination, emphasizing specific job skills over aptitude, and their own incompetence when it comes to retaining employees.

Age Discrimination

Norman Matloff, a computer science professor at U.C. Davis, claims that the there are plenty of workers available. According to Matloff, "It's simply impossible to reconcile the claims of a 'desperate labor shortage' with the fact that with many companies, perhaps only 2 percent of applicants are being hired. If they were as desperate as they claim, they just would not be as picky in their hiring as they are."[33]

Why are they being picky? Matloff says, "Because they don't want to pay the salaries . . . it's a matter of cost."[34] In other words, corporations are being

[33] *"There is No Desperate Labor Shortage,"* Wired News Report *(February 25, 1998)*

[34] *Ibid.*

selective because they don't want to pay experienced workers what they're worth.

Let's look at Microsoft. In *The Microsoft Way*, a book by Randall Stross, the author states that "Microsoft hires an almost infinitesimal sliver of the 120,000+ candidates who submit resumes each year." Stross also mentions Bill Gates' preference towards hiring recent college graduates. In 1994, when the average age of a Microsoft employee was 31, Gates expressed the desire to raise the percentage of workers hired directly from college to 80 percent.

If corporations have a goal with respect to employees, it's that they want to make you into an interchangeable cog. This way, it's easier for them to displace you with a cheaper substitute when the time comes.

Robert Cringley, in an excellent online commentary for PBS,[35] warned that

> *If a U.S. employer said out loud, "Gosh, we have a lot of 50-something engineers who are going to kill us with their retirement benefits so we'd better get rid of a few thousand," they would be violating a long list of labor and civil rights laws. But if they say, "Our cost of doing business in the U.S. is too high, so we'll be moving a few thousand jobs to India," that's just fine—even though it means exactly the same thing.*

Tim Jackson wrote a book entitled *Inside Intel*. In Chapter 35 there is a reference to *bumping*, "the practice, suggested to Intel by management consultants who feared that the company was aging too fast, of easing older employees out of the company and replacing them with younger ones."

Aren't those management consultants great? That's right, axe all of the older workers and feed them to the wolves; to hell with loyalty, hard work, and devotion. As long as they get their pound of flesh, those high-end strategic planning consultants don't care who has to take it in the neck. So what if older employees have valuable experience that separates them from recent college graduates?

In May 22, 1996, a representative from FACE Intel, Ken Hamidi, made the following inquiry at Intel's annual stockholder's meeting: "Please explain the downsizing policies and practices of Intel and how they increase profitability?" Craig Barret, Intel's COO at the time, is quoted as responding, "The half-life of an engineer, software, hardware engineer is only a few years. . . ."

Thus, acquiring experience cuts both ways. Sure, you might make yourself more valuable, but the minute that your salary actually increases you become a target for the efficiency experts. In Jackson's account, a field sales engineer named Bill Handel found himself under attack because he was "a forty-year-old sales engineer earning over $100,000 a year." Handel sued Intel, claiming age discrimination. After realizing that Intel would bankrupt him with legal opposition, he settled out of court.

[35] *Robert Cringley, "Body Count: Why Moving to India Won't Really Help IT," PBS (August 7, 2003)*

NOTE Folks, this isn't just some small aberration. Intel is arguable one of the largest public high-tech corporations on the planet. This is how things are done at a Fortune 100 multinational.

If you ever meet an Intel employee, ask them about the "ranking and rating" system (known by insiders as "ranting and raving"). In ranking and rating, a supervisor labels their subordinates as "outstanding," "successful," or "improvement required." Managers are sometimes under quota to have so many "improvement required" rankings, and in a group of "outstanding" employees they might have to rotate who gets the bad review.

Have you ever seen the movie *Cool Hand Luke*?

"Now why'd you shovel all that there dirt in my hole?"

For fun, look and see what kind of angst-ridden facial contortions an Intel employee makes when you mention the "Corrective Action Procedure (CAP)." A CAP is a procedure in which an employee is given a certain amount of time in which to fix whatever problems management is unhappy with. If they fail to succeed, they are fired. A vindictive manager might insist on completely unrealistic goals, which are intended to get an employee to quit out of frustration.

Skill Set Hypocrisy

Another thing that Matloff points out is that there's a certain degree of hypocrisy going on with respect to hiring. Matloff states that "Bill Gates has said that we should not be hiring on the basis of skills experience, that we should look for bright people. Jim McCarthy, one of Microsoft's top managers, has written in his book that we should not be hiring on the basis of skills, and yet that's precisely what Microsoft does."[36]

In Stross's book, *The Microsoft Way*, the hiring process at the company is described as placing a premium on raw intelligence. Specifically, "Microsoft's recruiting policies are designed with unapologetic single-mindedness to find others among the smartest."

As an experiment, let's look at the undergraduate computer science curriculum at the University of Illinois at Urbana-Champaign and compare it against a job posting at Monster.com.

A B.S. in computer science, concentrating in general engineering, would have a course sequence that looks like this:

Core requirements:

Math 120 Calculus & Analytic Geometry I
Chem 101 General Chemistry
Chem 105 General Chemistry Lab

---

[36] *"There is No Desperate Labor Shortage,"* Wired News Report *(February 25, 1998)*

Math 130 Calculus and Analytic Geometry II
CS 125 Introduction to Computer Science
CS 173 Discrete Mathematical Structures
Phycs 111 Mechanics

Math 242 Calculus and Analytic Geometry III
Math 225 Introductory Matrix Theory
CS 273 Introduction to Theory of Computation
Phycs 112 Electricity and Magnetism

CS 231 Computer Architecture
CS 225 Data Structures & Software Principles
Math 285 Differential Equations
Phycs 113 Fluids and Thermodynamics

CS 232 Computer Architecture II
CS 257 Numerical Methods
Math 361 Theory of Probability I
Phycs 114 Quantum Physics

CS 323 Operating System Design
ECE 205 Electricity & Electronic Circuits
ECE 206 Electricity & Electronic Circuits Lab
CS 321 Programming Languages & Compilers

Concentration requirements:

Math 315 Linear Transformations and Matrices (3)
TAM 152 Engineering Mechanics I—Statics (3)
TAM 212 Engineering Mechanics II—Dynamics (3)
G E 222 Introduction to Control Systems (4)
G E 324 Digital Control of Dynamic Systems (4)
G E 370 Introduction to Robotics (2)

Now let's look at a typical job posting (I searched under the job category of "Computer, Software" in "California-San Francisco"):

```
Applications Developer
Description:
Position is for a solid applications developer. The
application is mostly JavaScript, it is core to the
architecture, and not just a means to implement UI. There
will also be strong usage of SQL to be able to obtain
and modify data within the database. XML, XSL, and HTML
experience is also needed. Experience with source
control (specifically Clear Case) and bug databases (Clear
Quest) are important, as well as the ability to learn and
understand a given architecture
```

```
Requirements:
Required Experience: Apache Web server, Applications and
Tools, Applications Architecture, Communication, HTML, IBM
Rational, Clear Case, Information Technology, Internet,
Intranet, IP (Internet Protocol), Japanese, JavaScript,
JDBC (Java Database Connectivity), Oracle, Oracle Database
8i, Oracle Database 9i, Programmer, Software Developer,
Software Engineer, Solaris, Sun, TCP/IP, TOAD, UNIX,
Windows, and Written Communications.

Location: Belmont, CA
Pay Rate: DOE
Ref ID: 302539-2328-12-90837
```

Skill sets versus aptitude. Do you see "B.S. in computer science preferred" anywhere? Or how about "knowledge of discrete mathematical structures desired"? This is one reason why software companies are picky; they have a misplaced emphasis on skill sets. The truth is, *any monkey with half a brain can learn things like XML or JDBC*. Getting a degree in computer science from Urbana, on the other hand, takes a significant amount of ability and dedication. CS graduates have a strong foundation, and they're flexible; they can learn new things quickly.

These attributes offer CS graduates a greater possible range of expertise, in more depth, than some mailroom flunky who picked up a book on Visual C# in their spare time.

Unfortunately, the HR people just don't get this. Most HR managers are clueless about technology, and so they don't recognize the difference between a top-shelf computer science major and a part-time code monkey who's sexed-up their resume. The "shortage" results from this fact: *They have a harder time finding people because they're trying to match a grocery list of acronyms that they don't understand.*

The Retention Problem

Peter Cappelli is director of Wharton's Center for Human Resources. In 2003, he wrote an article in *Organizational Dynamics* 32, no. 3 entitled, "Will There Really Be a Labor Shortage?" Cappelli's study demonstrates that there won't be, demographically speaking, a shortage of American workers. Back when the *Social Security Act of 1935* (Public Law 271, 74th Congress) was passed, the life expectancy of the average person was around 64.[37] Social Security doesn't kick in until a person reaches 65, so the federal government probably thought that payouts wouldn't amount to much (heck, most people in 1935 would be dead before they hit 70 anyway).

---

[37] *National Center for Health Statistics*, National Vital Statistics Report *51, no. 3 (December 19, 2002)*

According to the National Center for Health Statistics, the life expectancy of the average American in 2001 was 77. With advances in medical technology and nutrition, this number will only increase. People are living over a decade longer than they used to. Given that most jobs in the U.S. are now in the service sector, where physical labor isn't a serious component, people are working longer. It's not just because they like to work either. Social Security is expected to start giving out more than it collects from taxpayers by 2017. People realize that they might be on their own, and they plan accordingly.

Donald Rumsfeld, the current Secretary of Defense, is way past 65. Warren Buffet, the investment deity, is in his 70s and shows no signs of slowing down. Carl Lindner, CEO of American Financial Group, makes Buffet look young. Lindner is in his 80s. In a Booz-Allen study that surveyed 2,500 public corporations, the average age for a CEO across all industries was 50 when they entered office.[38]

Now let's return to the numbers I analyzed in Chapter 4. If we change the working age range from 20–55 to 20–65, the percentage of the population that's working dramatically increases (see Table 5-3).

Table 5-3 Percentage of Working Population by Age Group

Range	2002	2010
0–19	28	27
20–64	50	60
65–100	22	13

Given that the demand for labor in 2010 is estimated to be at 168 million, we will easily meet this number (180 million, 60 percent of 300 million). *The offshoring proponents were so keen to stick to an artificial ceiling (55) that they neglected to account for old people who might want, or need, to work.*

Shame on you McKinsey Global Institute! Shame on you!

You management consultants are so eager to undermine our middle class that you fell back on a flawed argument!

What Cappelli concluded was that labor shortages were driven by turnover. Which is to say that most large companies have such miserable internal mechanisms to retain employees that people are leaving faster than HR can recruit them.

Not Enough Engineers

Although less than 5 percent of the 1.2 million undergraduates who received degrees in 2000–2001 were (strictly speaking) engineers, this doesn't count the other hard sciences. There were over 200,000 students in 2000–2001 who

[38] *Wendy Todaro, "Want to Be a CEO? Stay Put!"* Forbes.com *(March 31, 2003,* `http://www.forbes.com/2003/03/31/cx_wt_0401exec.html`*)*

received degrees in the hard sciences, approximately 16 percent of the total[39] (see Table 5-4).

Table 5-4 Hard Science Undergraduate Degrees in 2000–2001

Discipline	Graduates
Biological sciences/life sciences	60,553
Computer and information sciences	41,954
Engineering	58,098
Engineering-related technologies	13,922
Mathematics	11,674
Physical sciences and science technologies	17,979
Total	**204,180**

Furthermore, the National Center for Education Statistics in the *Projections of Education Statistics to 2013*[40] states that, between 2000–2001 and 2012–2013, the number of bachelor degrees granted will increase by 21 percent (this is the middle alternative projection) and the number of master degrees granted will increase by 19 percent.

Given my own experience, I would be tempted to say that students in the hard sciences may have a hard time finding work, regardless of what "experts" say about labor shortages. When I graduated from Cornell in 1992 with a B.A. in physics, absolutely no one (and I mean NO ONE) needed me. After four years of school and tens of thousands of dollars of tuition payments, I was hoping to do something related to math or science. Instead, I waited tables for three years until I could make it back to graduate school and acquire skills in a different area (and only then could I find a job).

David M. Lee, a senior physics professor at Cornell and a 1996 Nobel Prize winner, confided in me that "We have a hell of a time trying to find work for our Ph.D.s." These are top-shelf research scientists we're talking about, from a world-renowned university. They have a hard time finding work. Isn't there supposed to be a shortage?

Do you get the feeling that there's something fishy going on?

Offshoring proponents claim that we have a shortage of science and mathematics graduates. Where were all these people when I needed a job? Hmmm? I'd say that 99.9 percent of the high-tech employers don't need quantum field theory, they could care less about Gram-Schmidt orthogonalization, and they don't give a damn about combinatorial optimization. We're all overqualified as it is.

---

[39] *U.S. Department of Education, National Center for Education Statistics,* Digest of Education Statistics *(2002):Table 265*

[40] `http://nces.ed.gov//programs/projections/`

The labor shortage is an excuse, that's all it is, an excuse. They simply don't want to pay us what we're worth in the U.S. market. The "shortage" exists because the corporations can't find any American IT workers who'll work for $10,000 a year. Those corporate mouthpieces are all a self-serving bunch of inveterate weasels.

The Self-Fulfilling Prophesy

The sad part of offshore outsourcing is that, if it continues unbridled, it will create the very job shortage that corporations use as an excuse to go offshore in the first place. Offshore outsourcing will result in a self-fulfilling prophecy. As corporations send software jobs offshore, the demand for engineers in the U.S. will decrease (American engineers will simply be too expensive relative to their counterparts overseas). American college students will look around, see what's going on, and move into other fields. After a decade or so of this, we won't have a software industry in the U.S. because no American in their right mind will want to study it, since no one will hire them.

When this happens, who do you suppose will be writing the software that makes up the guidance system of our cruise missiles? Yes Virginia, it's a national security issue.

The Myth of the Free Market

We annually spend on military security more than the net income of all United States corporations.

—Dwight D. Eisenhower, farewell address, January 17, 1961

The money that's funneled through the Pentagon system is just a straight gift to the corporate manager, it's like saying, "I'll buy anything you produce, and I'll pay for research and development, and if you can make any profits, fine."

—Noam Chomsky, *Understanding Power*

Recall the definition that I gave in the last chapter. A *free market* economy is one in which buyers and sellers are allowed to engage in exchange based on prices that are reached through mutual agreement, *in the absence of government intervention*.

NOTE In practice, the ideal free market is a rare species. Thus, most free market advocates seek as little government intervention as possible.

Offshoring proponents claim that if we interfere with the free market that we'll become lazy and complacent; that the absence of competitive pressures will hamper innovation. When it comes to offshoring, the government needs to stand back and let nature take its course. This is what's best for the U.S. economy.

Unfortunately, there's something that these people aren't telling you. The truth is that we don't have a free market in the U.S. Hell, anyone who says that we have a free market economy in the U.S. is telling you a whopper! In terms of tax dollars spent, we have more government intervention in our economy than any other economy on the planet (take another look at Eisenhower's quote). All you have to do to see this is to look at how our tax money is spent, who gets funded, and which industries the government protects.

Our national government has a long history of protecting American industries. Protective tariffs, as it turns out, were a major impetus behind the Civil War. In the early 1800s, the South was an agrarian economy that exported much of its cotton overseas in exchange for cheap European goods. The Northern states, on the other hand, wanted protection from these same cheap European imports so that they could grow their own local manufacturing businesses. The North, via their representatives in the legislature, enacted the *Protective Tariff Law of 1828*. The South was nonplussed, and it referred to this law as the "Tariff of Abominations." Congress reduced these tariffs in 1932, but the South wasn't satisfied. In November 1932, the state of South Carolina passed the *Ordinance of Nullification*, which forbid the collection of tariffs.[41] South Carolina threatened to cede if the national government attempted to enforce its tariff laws, an omen of things to come.

According to the 2003 Federal budget, 368 billion dollars was allocated for the Department of Defense. This is about 18 percent of the total budget (2.1 trillion dollars, see Tables S-1 and S-2 in the budget document[42]). Thus, almost 20 percent of our tax base is going to companies like Lockheed, Boeing, and General Dynamic, many of which would not be able to survive in a truly "free market." For example, in the early 1970s, Lockheed was headed for bankruptcy. Guess who bailed them out? Yep, you guessed it, the U.S. federal government on behalf of the Nixon Administration. If a free market had actually existed, the government would have sat quietly in the background and let nature takes its course. Thanks to government spending (i.e., think AC-130), Lockheed doesn't have to worry about competing in a "free market."

IBM wouldn't be the monolith that it is today if it hadn't been for the U.S. Federal Government. During the 1950s, the U.S. government was IBM's largest customer. That's because computers were so expensive back then that anyone without a federal-sized budget couldn't afford one. Instead of relying on the free market to control costs, U.S. taxpayers footed the bill. In 1954,

---

[41] *Margaret E. Wagner (Editor), Gary W. Gallagher (Editor), Paul Finkelman (Editor), Library of Congress, James M. McPherson,* Library of Congress Civil War Desk Reference *(Simon & Schuster, 2002)*

[42] *U.S. Government Printing Office,* Budget of the U.S. Government, Fiscal Year 2003 *(2002): pp. 395, 396*

IBM completed the Naval Ordnance Research Computer (NORC) for the U.S. Navy Bureau of Ordnance. NORC was the fastest computer of its day. In 1958, IBM completed work on the Semi-Automatic Ground Environment (SAGE). SAGE was the first computer-based air-defense system that IBM manufactured for the Air Force.

In 1953, IBM unveiled the 701 Electronic Data Processing Machine. The 701 was originally referred to as the "Defense Calculator," given that the U.S. Government had requested a machine for use in the design of aircrafts and the development of nuclear devices. Customers of the 701 include the National Security Agency, the U.S. Navy, and the U.S. Weather Bureau.[43]

NOTE Show me an industry in our economy that's doing well, and I'll show you an industry in our economy that has a large government sector.

In 1994, John Meriwether founded a hedge fund named Long Term Capital Management (LTCM) in Greenwich, Connecticut. Meriwether, as described in Michael Lewis's *Liar's Poker*, was a legendary trader who built his reputation at Solomon Brothers. On the board were two soon-to-be Nobel Prize winners, Robert Merton and Myron Scholes. Merton and Scholes were awarded the Nobel Prize in Economics three years later, in 1997, for their work on option pricing models.

Shrouded in secrecy, LTCM was able to achieve an annual rate of return of 40 percent. By the end of 1997, the hedge fund had $4.8 billion in capital and $120 billion in assets. In 1998, when the Russian government defaulted on its debt, the bottom dropped out and LTCM lost over half of its capital. By September 19, 1998, the company had only $600 million in capital and assets of $80 billion. On September 20, officials from the U.S. Treasury department and the New York Federal Reserve made a Sunday visit to LTCM to have a look-see. The Federal Reserve ended up arranging a bailout of LTCM that involved a consortium of 14 different financial institutions. Instead of letting nature takes it course, the government intervened and came to the aid of an ailing LTCM.

Our invasion of Iraq has proven to be a gold rush to companies like Goodyear and Boeing, one that has been funded courtesy of the U.S. taxpayer. For example, Bradley fighting vehicles in Iraq wear through their tracks in about 60 days. New tracks cost $22,576 per vehicle. In 2003, the U.S. military burned through $230 million just paying for new tracks. This is triple the 2002 figure of $78 million.[44]

The Army has already consumed $1.3 billion in replacement parts for its helicopters and aircrafts. Boeing, in particular, stands to make a nice chunk of change supplying replacement parts for the Apache attack helicopter. In 2003,

[43] `http://www-1.ibm.com/ibm/history/exhibits/701/701_customers.html`

[44] *Jonathan Weisman and Renae Merle, "Wearing Out and Adding Up,"* Washington Post *(September 13, 2003)*

the Army burned through $200 million worth of helicopter blades, four times the normal amount.[45]

> *What we're seeing is waste and gold-plating that's enriching Halliburton and Bechtel while costing taxpayers billions of dollars and actually holding back the pace of reconstruction in Iraq.*[46]
>
> —Representative Henry Waxman (D-California)

Halliburton has billions in government contracts and is the largest private contractor in Iraq. This is a company whose once CEO is now the Vice President of the United States. Halliburton's engineering arm (Kellogg, Brown and Root, or KBR) was awarded a noncompetitive $7 billion contract with the Army Corps of Engineers to restore Iraq's oil fields and an $8.6 billion contract to provide logistical support for the Army.[47]

Halliburton has also been found guilty of overcharging on a number of occasions. Specifically, the company overcharged the federal government by $27.4 million in a contract to feed troops and $61 million in a contract to import gasoline.[48] Once more, two KBR employees were found to have accepted up to $6 million in kickbacks from a Kuwaiti company, leading to even more overcharges.[49] Shortly after the disclosure of the kickbacks, the Army Corps of Engineers gave Halliburton yet another contract for oil restoration work valued at $1.2 billion.[50]

Can you spell "w-a-r p-r-o-f-i-t-e-e-r-i-n-g?"

What exists is a thinly veiled double standard. The federal government funnels subsidies, contracts, tax breaks, depreciation allowances, and regulatory cutbacks to a select group of corporations. The free market is great for the average American worker. Displaced American workers can be harshly lectured on the need for self-reliance and independence by self-righteous (and sometimes drug-addled) political commentators. For corporate executives, however, the welfare state must thrive.

So, if we don't really have a free market, why do all these executives prattle on about it? Well, the corporate elite uses the free market argument because it's a convenient ideological weapon that they can wield against things like social spending (which they derisively refer to as "entitlements") or anything else that might constrain their ability to generate profits. They wield it when it suits their purposes. When you suggest cuts in defense spending, however, these same people jump to their feet in protest.

---

[45] *Ibid.*

[46] *Jonathan Weisman and Anitha Reddy, "Spending on Iraq Sets Off Gold Rush,"* Washington Post *(October 9, 2003)*

[47] *Douglas Jehl, "Pentagon Finds Halliburton Overcharged on Iraq Contracts,"* New York Times *(December 11, 2003)*

[48] *Peter Carlson, "The Profitable Connections Of Halliburton,"* Washington Post *(February 10, 2004)*

[49] *"Halliburton Admits $6m Kickbacks,"* BBC News *(January 23, 2004)*

[50] *Larry Margasak, "Army Changes Explanation on Halliburton,"* Associated Press *(February 10, 2004)*

The Fundamental Issue

The public be damned.

—William H. Vanderbilt

A corporation is a legal entity. It doesn't possess an inherent sense of patriotism or morality. Corporations exist to do one thing: generate profits. Transnational corporations like GE are colossal machines that lumber from country to country, mindlessly chewing up the landscape and leaving piles of currency in their wake—giant green confetti dung heaps. There is no right or wrong. There are only the accounting concepts of profit and loss.

So when you hear someone talk about "greedy multinational corporations," it's nonsensically redundant. It can only be expected that corporations want to make money, as much as they can within the confines of the law; it's their nature. The digestive track of a corporation is eternally hungry.

Given that corporations exist to make money, patriotism is a PR issue, one that is usually solved with a few charitable contributions or maybe by buying some airtime during a sporting event. Multinationals in particular owe no loyalty to any country outside of the taxes that they pay and the laws that they must observe. Hell, some multinationals, like IBM with over 300,000 employees, are their own little sovereignty.

The only group of individuals that a company is responsible to is its shareholders. Everyone else can dangle when it comes to turning a profit. CEOs don't swear allegiance to political leaders. Oh no, it's the other way around. Presidents, prime ministers, and chancellors all bow down to the corporate deities. Who do you think makes all those campaign contributions?[51]

In light of all this, the emergence of offshoring raises a question:

Is what's good for corporations also good for the American public?

When it comes to offshore outsourcing, this is what everyone is really haggling over. If American multinationals are focused on revenue and cost structure, are their resulting actions also in the best interest of the American public?

The corporations would have you believe that what's good for them is also good for you. Those well-paid MBA types at McKinsey (whose customers just happen to be large transnational corporations) refer to offshoring as a "win-win" scenario. Then again, McKinsey really doesn't have a choice, does it? To say otherwise would be to admit that what corporations are doing is wrong (from an ethical standpoint). Admitting to wrongdoing would cause McKinsey to lose its client base very quickly.

I believe that what's good for large multinationals is *not always* good for the U.S. as a whole. American history is rife with business leaders and corporations whose aims were at odds with the best interests of the general public. I'm talking about men like John D. Rockefeller, Theodore Vail, and Bill Gates.

---

[51] `http://www.opensecrets.org`

I'm talking about corporations like Standard Oil, AT&T, and Microsoft. Corporations are all about generating shareholder value, and this doesn't necessarily have anything to do with public welfare (especially when stock ownership is concentrated in a small percentage of the overall population).

End Game

> *What a stupendous, what an incomprehensible machine is man! Who can endure toil, famine, stripes, imprisonment & death itself in vindication of his own liberty, and the next moment . . . inflict on his fellow men a bondage, one hour of which is fraught with more misery than ages of that which he rose in rebellion to oppose.*
>
> —Thomas Jefferson to Jean Nicholas Demeunier, January 24, 1786

Since the late 1960s, the gap between the rich and the poor of this country has been getting wider. Wealth has become concentrated in fewer and fewer hands. Offshoring is one facet of this gradual polarization. In a book entitled *The State of Working America*, published by the Cornell University Press, the authors conclude that "while inequality grew more slowly in the 1990s than in the prior decade, the richest families continued to reap disproportionate gains."[52] The authors also state that "the wealthiest 1% of all households control about 38% of national wealth, while the bottom 80% of households hold only 17%."[53] Recall the 2001 SCF data collected by the Federal Reserve. The top 10 percent of the income spectrum increased their net assets by 35 percent from 1998 to 2001.

As the wealth accumulates at the top of the income spectrum, so does power. Like it or not, as things stand now, the people who control this country are the same people who control the capital. Through product sponsorship, campaign contributions, and corporate grants, the privileged few are able to manipulate both our media and our political system (see Figure 5-1).

The elite are livestock farmers by trade and the rest of us are sheep. They use the media to shepherd us where they want us to go. They fleece us every so often (right around April 15). They send us to the slaughterhouse. They even experiment on us without our knowledge.[54] Don't believe me? If you have some spare time on the weekends, take a look at the Tuskegee Syphilis experiments[55] or the U.S. military's Project 112.[56]

---

[52] *Lawrence Mishel, Jared Bernstein, and Heather Boushey,* The State of Working America 2002/2003 *(Cornell University Press, 2003)*

[53] *Ibid.*

[54] *Robert Gehrke, "Pentagon Withholds Cold War Medical Data,"* Associated Press *(January 16, 2004)*

[55] *James H. Jones,* Bad Blood Tuskegee Syphilis Experiment *(Free Press, 1993)*

[56] `http://deploymentlink.osd.mil/current_issues/shad/shad_intro.shtml`

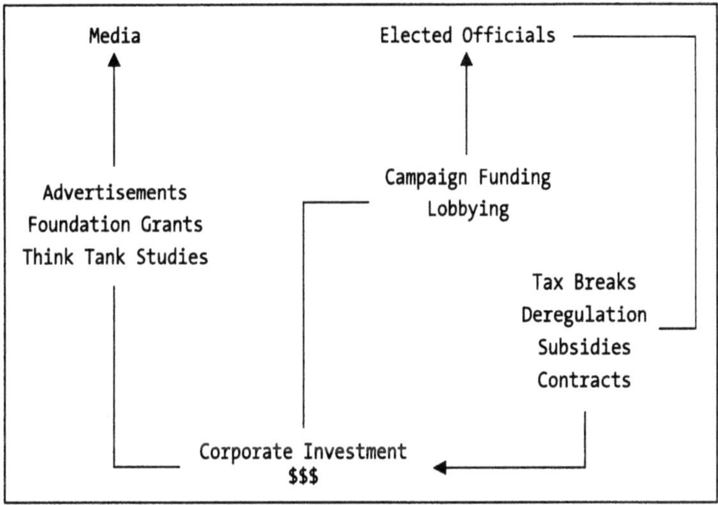

Figure 5-1 How the elite maintain control

They own us through debt and they make the rules as they see fit. Open up the dictionary sometime and look up the word *husbandry*. When you're done with that, look up the word *cull*.

As the wealthy amass more influence and power, the multinational corporations that represent them will purchase a greater share of influence in our domestic and foreign policies. The decisions that get made (e.g., taxing, spending, regulation) will reflect their best interest. Wars won't be fought in the name of the people, but in the name of a prevailing corporate axis. Bear in mind the history of humankind, since the dawn of civilization, can be defined in terms of groups of people competing for resources. Who's to say that we'll ever change?

Inevitably, corporations will become so large and influential that they supersede national governments. This is the end game of globalization. Already, there are institutions like Citigroup whose net assets ($1.2 trillion) come very close to the annual GDP of a developed country like France ($1.558 trillion, 2002 est.). The authority of nation-states will, little by little, be eroded away. When this happens, my bet is that a loose consortium of global corporate entities will loom quietly in the background, a much more efficient, low-key, and private version of the U.N. It doesn't have to be overt. No new flags will be raised. Corporate interests will merely treat the government as an intermediary, through which they indirectly implement their plans and pursue their own best interests.

What Can I Possibly Do?

We hold these truths to be self-evident: that all men are created equal. . .
—*Declaration of Independence*, July 4, 1776

Reality is depressing. Most of us are but specks in the grand scheme of things. We live our lives, and die, and the world keeps on spinning, oblivious to our fate. It's as if we hadn't been here at all. How can an average Joe possibly defy the cumulative will of large multinational corporations? The proponents liken offshoring to entropy; it's inevitable, they say. Do you dare to disturb the natural order of things?

People like me can jump up and down trying to get the truth out, but none of my spastic gyrations will matter until you, dear reader, get up and do something about it. That begs a question, doesn't it? What should you do?

It's not hopeless. The entrenched power structure isn't invulnerable. Progress has been made. Groups of normal, everyday people have been able to institute broad changes in our society—changes that benefited large segments of out population. The first one that comes to mind is the Civil Rights Movement. Also, don't think for a minute that the Vietnam protests didn't have something to do with our eventual withdrawal. Former CIA agent John Stockwell states, "The youth did rise up and stop the Vietnam War."[57]

NOTE You can find out more about the CIA in Stockwell's book, *In Search of Enemies*.

Politics is all about inertia. A large portion of the voting public doesn't vote. According to the U.S. Federal Election Commission, in 2000 only 105,586,274 (67.5 percent) of the 156,421,311 people registered to vote actually went to the vote.[58] On top of that, 100,228,726 members of the voting age population aren't even registered to vote! This means that only about half of the people who can vote end up voting.

Perhaps people are disgusted with politics. I don't blame them. They figure, "Hey, if I vote, it only encourages them and provides them more legitimacy." Nevertheless, if these nonvoters got to the booth on Election Day, and voted with their conscience, our system would have the opportunity to change.

The trick, of course, is to ignore the media. Ignore the polls. Ignore the pundit who warns you that you're wasting your vote. The media has been bought and paid for.

---

[57] `http://www.thirdworldtraveler.com/Stockwell/StockwellCIA87_2.html`

[58] `http://www.fec.gov/pages/2000turnout/reg&to00.htm`

If history has shown anything, it's that the majority has an ace up its sleeve: sheer numbers. Simply put, there's a lot more of us than there is of them. In a democratic society, that's supposed to mean something (all people are created equal, etc.). Thus, to affect change, you'll need to become politically active and encourage others to do the same. I'm not saying that you have to handcuff yourself to a tree and become a vegetarian; I'm talking about *taking the time to vote and supporting candidates who reflect your values*. Start by taking responsibility for your own actions, and then move on from there.

Index

Numbers

A

B

F

G

H

J

S

T

U

V

GPSR Compliance
The European Union's (EU) General Product Safety Regulation (GPSR) is a set of rules that requires consumer products to be safe and our obligations to ensure this.

If you have any concerns about our products, you can contact us on

ProductSafety@springernature.com

In case Publisher is established outside the EU, the EU authorized representative is:

Springer Nature Customer Service Center GmbH
Europaplatz 3
69115 Heidelberg, Germany

www.ingramcontent.com/pod-product-compliance
Ingram Content Group UK Ltd.
Pitfield, Milton Keynes, MK11 3LW, UK
UKHW051126260726
13967UKWH00010B/2889
* 9 7 8 1 4 3 0 2 5 3 0 8 2 *